HORROR In The WOODS

True Stories

Steph Young

Table of Contents

Introduction

In this volume, we have such wild-but-true stories as secret government documents allegedly arranging for the abduction of humans, aliens reported to be taking people in forests, an underground tunnel harbouring abducted children in a national park, invisible predators luring people into the woods to an unknown fate, a disappearance at a national park campground resulting in transportation to an experimental underground base, mass abductions, psychological warfare, experiments of torture, mind control, time travel and inter-dimensional travel, Reptilians and Greys, and a beast that cannot be defined....what more could we ask for?

Monsters, aliens, or Humans? ~ you decide.....

Chapter 1: Taken from the campground to a sinister underground base.

In 1971 when Michelle Guerin was a teenager, she was went missing from Ditch Plains Campground near Shadmoor State Park in Montauk, New York State.

'During a visit to my Uncle's campsite at Ditch Plains in Montauk, I went missing for 2-3 hours and my uncle remembers it.' It happened in 1971. Thirty-plus years later in 2003, she finally explained what happened to her, after she underwent hypnosis with a Dr. Kouguell to recover more of her memories about it. Memories had been coming back to her over the years, and they were far from pleasant. In fact, they were horrifying.

She recalls her arrival at the campsite. "We arrive and I change into my bathing suit. It's boring, so I'm going to look around. I

walk off and after a while I pass a group of surfers camping there. One of them looks familiar. It's "A" – "A's" brother. (She keeps other people's names out of it for confidentiality.) He asks if I've seen "…" yet – he says he's surfing. So, I decide to walk down to look for him in the water.

I spot him and when he heads in from the water he calls my name. He asks if I want to take a walk later and can I meet him back at the campsite. So, later I'm at the campsite with him and we start walking, for about just under a mile and then we walk into the dunes to find a quiet spot. There's a cliff and tall grass.

We sit down on his towel and start making-out, laying down. Suddenly I hear a loud buzzing like lots of bees. We sit up. What is this? Something's not right! We should run away! I try to yell but I can't talk. I can't move! I want my Mom.'

'It sounds like a car is coming then stops. The buzzing is louder. A man in a soldier's uniform is looking down at me. Another soldier kicks "A." He says, "He's out of it." There are two others with him. They pick me up. They carry "A" like firemen.

We're in a jeep going through grass. There's a hill up ahead. The hill is moving! – it looks like there is a door in the hill. It moves. We drive inside. Other men in black berets are inside. "A" is held by two men. Two take me. We go through a door into a bright hallway and turn right into another hallway. At another hallway, "A" is still going straight but we stop at an elevator.

Inside, we're going down and then the door opens and it's much darker down here. There's a smell...like a cesspool. It's so cold. There's a door and one of the soldiers opens it. The room is so dark I can hardly see. It looks like there's a padded table. They lay me down on it. Then leave the room.'

'I can't seem to move anything but my eyes. Why am I here? I don't like this. Over to my left something moves. It's coming closer...I can see it better. OH MY GOD! It's a monster!'

'(Note: At this point I got so agitated I was almost jumping off the chair in the Dr's office. I can't stop crying and shaking. I had to be calmed down before I could continue.)'

'What I see is a creature, about 6-7 feet tall. Its ears are large and pointed. His eyes are bright yellow. They glow. It has pointed teeth. He has a tail. He's coming toward me.....I have never been so scared in all my life. He comes to the foot of the table. He pulls my bathing suit off....His face is so close to mine.... I hear raspy sounds.'

'He puts something inside me and I feel like I'm being ripped apart. He likes to see how terrified I am of him. It gives him a lot of pleasure...... When he is done, he goes back to the part of the room I first saw him in...'

'They help me from the room. I am taken to a well-lit room. There are machines I don't recognize. A table covered in white. Lots of stainless steel equipment. I am strapped down on that table. People come in wearing white gowns and masks. I feel a prick in my arm."

She remembers nothing after that, until she comes around, back at the beach. She also had recall of 'a dark cloaked figure.' 'I do not recall any facial features since it was obscured by a hood. I recalled an "interrogation" by some very human-looking men in military attire. I was asked questions about what I call "the little men" – the "greys."

One of their questions was; "Who," or, "What are they?" I replied; "They are us." After this session, I was stymied. This was not something I believed. If there is a relationship, I have yet to connect the dots.

I do not know why the beings I recalled did not appear to have souls."

Michelle wonders, "Have I fabricated this?" - 'I can certainly understand people questioning this. I still find myself questioning if it happened or if I fabricated it all. It was this scepticism that forced me to seek as much validation as I could.'

Is it suspicious, or simply unfortunate coincidence, that when scheduled to speak about her experience in November 1991, she suffered a stroke two days before this?

She has had other flashbacks about this time when she was taken from the campground, including seeing a face of a person and a conversation that seemed to be telepathic, of 'him' calling her "little one," and attempting to soothe her.

'I recall being in a dark place, afraid, floating in something that felt heavier than water. I had been standing naked in front of

a metal door, struggling with a soldier while a doctor told me I had to do it. I was pleading with him not to make me go in there... I am afraid of drowning. I want to get out. Why do I have to be in here? I calm myself enough to float. I can feel wires attached to me. I stretch out my arms trying to feel the walls that enclose me.'

'Are my eyes open? Blackness, floating motion. I can see movement, shadows and forms. Dark grey now. "Don't be afraid little one, take my hand, I will guide you."

'Grey turns to blue like the sky, white clouds. It feels like I'm flying. I see tranquil blue water, a beautiful lush hill, mountainous area, deep canyons. A big white building. Diving through the white foam of a deep blue wave. I am underwater. I can see a dark entrance to a cave among the rocks and hills. It is a desolate place.'

'I feel lonely, cold, time is not what we think it is. Each moment is happening now. An endless loop that we can enter at many

points but we should take care not to disrupt the loops.'

Where Michelle was abducted is the same area as the infamous 'Montauk.' On the Eastern tip of Long Island, New York State, lies an isolated, desolate stretch of land. It's now owned by the New York State Office of Parks & Recreations. What remains now of the former Military Base once operational there, is a huge radar dish, abandoned outbuildings, and bunkers. When it was abandoned, it became a ripe place for urban explorers, although many found it to be a creepy place to venture into, as well as risky in terms of safety and the possibility of getting caught for trespassing.

It's not the over-ground remains of the buildings there that most intrigue; it's what lies underground, or what is alleged to have. One of the most widely held beliefs is that the former Air force base comprises of facilities under the ground amid an

elaborate network of subterranean tunnels, and some believe it is still operational beneath the ground, and is home to top-secret and nefarious black ops projects and experiments. Some parts of the camp remained closed off and guarded still supposedly, especially the areas near the old satellite and military installations.

Richard Whelan, vice president of the East Hampton Trails Preservation Society and a military history buff, interviewed by Sagharbor Express, said he has explored Camp Hero in depth over the years, before it was legal to do so and afterwards.

"There's nothing behind it; there is no mystery. To the people who live here, it's just about selling books..." he says dismissively.

Interestingly though, the deeds to Camp Hero state that although the above-ground belongs to the Office of Parks and

Recreation, everything below-ground belongs to the Government, and those who are termed "conspiracy researchers," think there is a lot more to Camp Hero than this local historian says. Most notably, there are more 'witnesses' than just Michelle who would disagree with Whelan's benign version of the story of camp Hero. These 'witnesses' say they were taken and held underground, and the circumstances were far from pleasant.

It's an alleged place of mass child abductions, psychological warfare, experiments of torture, mind control, time travel and inter-dimensional travel, Reptilians and Greys, and a beast that cannot be defined.

If we go back to Michelle's experience of being abducted near her Uncle's campsite and allegedly taken underground where she was placed in a room with a 'monster,' Dr.

Helmut Lammer PhD, who wrote 'MILABS: Military Mind Control & Alien Abduction' in 2000, attempts to dissect her experience at Montauk.

'We don't think that the military worked with this reptoid creature. It could be possible that she was drugged with a hallucinogen, raped by a human, and the reptoid projected as a kind of screen memory... although she described the skin and other features of the creature quite realistically...'

Adding to this theory, researcher Dr. Stanislav Grof wrote that the strange alien worlds drugged LSD subjects discover and explore seem to have a reality of their own, although not in the range of our cosmos; 'they appear to exist in other dimensions or in universes coexistent with ours. The drugged individuals can encounter 'entities' who have bizarre physical forms.'

He cites that one female of his LSD experiencers had a sense of identification with a species of large reptiles. While experiencing this, she opened her eyes and looked at the therapist, "who seemed transformed into a reptile too. She was fascinated by scales she visualized on the side of the therapist's head."

Since many people have phobias about reptiles, Dr. Lammer theorises that it could thus be logical that they could experience such beings if they were on a drug trip. 'It should be clear then that Michelle's reptoid/rape experience could have been drug induced, where she possibly saw a human transformed into a 'reptoid,' like some of these drugged test subjects.

He goes further; 'After the attack on her, Michelle was escorted to an examination room and strapped down. After this examination, she was forced into an

isolation tank where she began to hallucinate. Declassified documents show that intelligence agencies had great interest in this research and used hallucinogens for cover stories to discredit individuals during covert operations.'

'We believe that her experience shows there is evidence she was a victim of such deprivation experiments. - If the abductee underwent hypno-program- ming by military psychiatrists, it should have been possible to create imaginary alien encounters.'

He also offers another alternative. 'A research project by Dr. Alvin Lawson and Dr. W. C. McCall led to a scientifically testable hypothesis that at least some "alien abduction" experiences are actually 'Birth Memories.' - prenatal or birth memories. This was mostly ridiculed by ET-proponents.'

'In an attempt to evaluate 'alien abductee' claims, these doctors induced imaginary abduction experiences in a team of volunteers who had demonstrated no significant knowledge of UFO's. Data from four imaginary and four real abduction cases showed no substantial differences.

Also, patterns echoing well-established details from real alien abduction encounters emerged from these imaginary sessions. All of the described incidents were identical with those in alien abductions, from 'disc-like crafts' 'humanoids,' 'aliens passing through solid walls,' were seen in the volunteers.

'In the birth-memory study (of Dr. Grof.) encounters are described with different types of non-human beings – 'foetal, animal, robot, creature, and apparitional. These types are close to the reported 'alien' beings' of real alien abductions.'
One test subject described: "...He sort of

has a scaly-like skin...I am not comfortable... the other scaly ones... they just seem to be sort of non-existent or guard-type things or something..."

'This imaginary abductee reported "reptoid non-human" beings on board an imaginary UFO. He was just as frightened as the 'real' abductees, like Michelle.'

Lammer adds that the research doctor was then very surprised to find that his research results led to an unusual reaction. Although the article he produced describing his experiments was published in a very obscure and little-read journal, he said that he immediately began to receive literally hundreds of requests for more detailed information from military research centres, worldwide.

He concludes; 'We should therefore be aware of the reported similarities between drug-induced hallucinations, and alien

abduction experiences! We can see from this imaginary 'alien abduction' study that it would be easy for psychiatrists who work for secret military or intelligence agencies to create 'alien abduction scenarios' that appear similar to 'real' abduction encounters.'

After he had written this article, he later attempted to discover if isolation tanks such as the one Michelle described being placed into in water, really could exist. Writing on Rense.com he says; 'I researched the literature on sensory deprivation experiments and came across isolation tanks invented by Dr. John Lilly. Dr. Lilly tried to find out how he could isolate the brain and mind. He found such a tank inside a soundproof chamber in an isolated building near the campus of the National Institute of Health.'

'This isolation tank was built during World War II for experiments by the Office of

Naval Research on underwater swimmers. This was the beginning of research on isolation, including with drugs.'

Crucially he also points out; 'It should be noted that Lilly was contacted by covert intelligence services for the Department of Defense. As the isolation tank research became known, various individuals from government agencies called him to find out about it. The doctor claims that among them were researchers working in 'brain-washing.' They asked him if the isolation tank could be used to 'change believe systems of persons under coercion.' They wanted to use the tanks for experiments in mind control and to 'brain-wash.'

'The Doctor visualized that peoples believe systems could be changed as desired by the controllers. He was convinced that military/intelligence would indeed use this isolation technique for covert experiments.'

'I think Michelle's experiences show us that this was true and that there is enough evidence that she is one victim of such a deprivation tank experiment. One should note, however, that this had nothing to do with aliens,' (- in Lammer's opinion, that is. Is he right?

Three years prior to Michelle's experience becoming known, a 'special report' by John Quinn, who ran 'Newshawk,' an e-mail based news service, was published in Volume 25, no: 13 of the Phoenix Journal, in October 1999.

'A man now living in Calgary named John Tooker has had substantial recall of personal involvement in the Montauk Project. John Tooker believes he was a participant during the Montauk Project operations in the late 1970's and early 1980's, while in an altered state of mind and/or in some alternate, parallel reality or "timeline."

'He says he was a very different person there, when he was working on advanced time technologies at the base; that is, that he literally may have been subjected to some kind of age regression and/or transfer of consciousness.'

'During this time he was also known as "Daniel John Waters," and he has reported on some very strange happenings in Calgary too, which sound similar to Denver, with Denver being as the centre for the 'NWO.') Given that Calgary is in roughly the same geographical relationship to the continental divide as is Denver, perhaps there is some esoteric/earth-energy relationship, which may make Calgary suitable for use as another NWO "nerve centre."

'He informed me that one base, although 'decommissioned' and 'closed,' (he says, 'here we go again'), is in fact, still functioning but has become extremely secretive. This is based on observation and

eye-witness testimony from a guard who'd been employed there. Just recently, this guard - a close friend of Tooker - and who has worked with him on some research' (- One could perhaps question this - Do security guards often work with physicists helping them with their research?! unless the writer Quinn means 'helped' with Tooker's research into the things going on at the base instead) 'was transferred without explanation from the location.'

'There was more notable weirdness' (bearing in mind this report was written in 1999 - almost two decades ago) 'which he told me was going on there; so-called phone transmitter towers appearing everywhere. There is a covert purpose in this, - such transmitters are being used for mind control and mind-modification of the population. Most towers are operating at much more power than is needed for just cell-phone transmissions.'

Quinn adds, 'My home is in a very sparsely populated mountain region. Sure enough, a transmitter was installed on the mountain.'

'I was told that Denver is literally crawling with 'Montauk boys' and, to an extent, 'Montauk girls'; these are young people with Aryan characteristics who have been programmed with Montauk/ Monarch techniques in order to be 'sleeper agents,' who are to be used in psychotic, satanic and murderous covert government "operations."

Bizarrely, Quinn also said the streets of Calgary have, (in 1999) 'become inundated with a tremendous number of street people, the great majority of whom fit the "requirements" for the typical 'Montauk Boys' to a tee.'
Is this all a little too conspiratorial and imaginative? Are the testimonies of better-known "Montauk boys," such as Al Bielik, Preston Nichols and Stewart

Swerdlow's vivid accounts of their time there absolutely believable, or sheer fantasy? - That would be for the reader to decide.

Quinn's report continues, as if, in his opinion, to confirm the reality of the Montauk project; 'Large portions of Long Island have underground facilities, including of course the Brookhaven Labs - confirmed to the Long Island reporter Jerry Cimisi by a private contractor who apparently worked often at the facility there.'

Of John Tooker, he appears to have been posting on the Internet since the time that John Quinn wrote his 1999 report revealing him as a "Montauk" experiencer. This is a post he made in 2002, to "John Titor," a person who had also come forward a few years ago to say he was posting messages from the future;

"You're a time traveller too? Have you ever interacted with any of the pre-1983 staff at Montauk? If so, you may have met me. When I was working there, I was a Research and Development assistant to Dr. Von Neumann, (a 'Project Paperclip' Nazi brought to America) and was known as Daniel John Waters. I had a rank of Lt. Col., in the Psi Corps."

Tooker (formerly known as Daniel John Waters) apparently says he helped Steven Gibbs build HDR units in the 1980's. Steven Gibbs created the 'HDR' or 'Hyper Dimensional Resonator,' in 1985. A device, in Gibbs words, apparently has the ability to send people physically through time.

Self-titled "Hoax-hunter," researcher John Rasmus believes John Tooker is a person connected with time travel but outside of the 'John Titor' story. Rasmus adds, "Tooker is clearly not sane... but few HDR users

are... He posts his personal home address constantly on his websites which are full of time travel links and stories of him being a "Montauk Boy." (These websites I believe are unfortunately no longer online.)

For a while, there was much speculation on forums as to whether Tooker was in fact actually 'John Titor,' although the 'John Titor - time traveller from the future' could be a hoax anyway. In fact, recently "John Titor" seems to have returned, but that's another story, and again, quite possibly a hoax too.

To add to this confusion, more recently, another person with a PhD has come forward to say he is the former "John Tooker" of Montauk, and that the Montauk base might have closed down, but the projects going on underground, simply moved. 'There is another John on the internet who does have my last name

(Tooker) that is also a supposed time traveller. What is interesting about this is that the project moved from Montauk to Robins Air Force Base in Warner Robins, GA in 1995. I moved from Tucson to Warner Robins in 1994 and graduated from high school there in 1998. Warner Robins is a small town and many people there know me as Jon.'

'I was working in the high strain-rate lab (at Georgia Tech). I had independently continued my cosmology research. If my work leads to free energy...but a spy came to look at what I was working on. There used to be a site online in 2004 or so-called John {my last name}'s time travel website but it is offline now. That other 'John' that does have my last name is credited with helping Steven Gibbs build the hyper-dimensional resonator, (who, under duress, later built one for a witch.)'

'While doing my PhD studies at Georgia

Tech I solved the major outstanding problem in physics. I was also very involved in the Occupy Atlanta movement and I believe it is (partially) for those political reasons (I was having strife with the local DHS agents) that I am not being given due credit for what is plainly evident in my research. You may recall the FBI released information about a plot to assassinate the 'Occupy' leaders.'

'Here is the first paper I wrote. It is highly technical but non-mathematical and very short. If you have some familiarity with physics I hope it is understandable. I believe I wrote this on the timeline both Titor's visited, in 2009 with a divergence of 1.941.'

He claims to have had his manuscripts rejected and plagiarised by academics, several times. He then adds, strangely, 'I looked exactly like Jack Parsons, (the

rocket scientist who some say was experimenting with Aleister Crowley) opening a portal to let entities into our world in that incarnation.'

He says; 'I discovered all this largely via recovered memories and psychical research but I have no hard evidence that this person existed. Which is why I'm trying to contact other time travellers. BTW, this isn't my original timeline, as I believe that I jumped timelines, not long after doing some work with Steve Gibbs, on his trip up to Calgary.'

A sceptical poster responds; 'So, while working on your PhD you were part of the Montauk Project, Steven Gibbs 'HDR' Project, you were working with Al Bielek, Dr. Von Newmann and you held the rank of Lt. Col working on the PSI Corps under a different name... and you wonder why your professors didn't take your physics theories seriously?'

Well, we will I think have to take this all with a pinch of salt.

Presumably no relation, but interestingly there happened to be a Liam Wallace Tooker who lived on Long Island, home of Montauk, (1848 – 1917.) This 'Tooker' is best known for his translations of Indian place names and his study of the first known inhabitants of Montauk; the aboriginal 'Montaukett' - a place name which the colonists conferred upon the tribal Indians there, and meaning 'Fort place.'

In 2012, the "Montauk Boy," John Tooker wrote; 'I am the anonymous physicist behind the black hole research. I am probably the time travel guy John Tooker. Seems likely "John Titor" is just disinformation. In John Quinn's article Camp Hero and the Montauk Project Today, he states that the project moved from Montauk to Warner Robins, GA in 1995.'

'I moved from Tucson to Warner Robins in 1994 when I was 13. John Quinn also mentions John Tooker by name in that article. How can I prove my identity? Idk... Here is a copy of my GT id:

I joined the Marines at 18. Got out, went to college. I was working on my PhD at Georgia Tech in 2009. I was a Presidential Fellow in the Center for Relativistic Astrophysics. My research quickly evolved into a solution to some other big mysteries and I wrote a paper about it.'

Many ridicule him in response to his posting, and say he copied from Wikipedia or that he's insane. Well, it's a difficult thing to decipher his theories and research, and certainly I'm not up to that task, but perhaps readers would like to take a look! Is it simply ramblings of an active imagination? And is Montauk really the stuff of science-fiction?

Well, there's also a lady called Jolene JoJo Seebacher who says she was also at Montauk. She says she is a survivor of medical experimentation, satanic ritual abuse, and Black Ops military mind programming. She says her abuse began while still in the womb, when her foetus was injected multiple times.

On James Bartley's radio show she says, "I was enhanced in my mother's womb. When I was born I was enhanced further. I was given thousands of injections in my early years and medicated through these injections. I was taken to my father's business, called " " pharmaceuticals. He had worked for this company in the food services side, where some of the Project Paperclip scientists (an alleged secret project involving Nazi scientists including Wernher von Braun recruited by the US Government during WWII.) were working and which later became Newhaven Labs

(Montauk's vast underground labs were supposed to be staffed by scientists from Brookhaven Laboratories.)

'During my childhood there I underwent terrible torture, terrible trauma and then testing. In that order. Torture-trauma-testing.

Torture-trauma-testing. My siblings got other treatments while I was delivered to their private "classes" and literally tortured.'

'Thrown in rooms, water boarded, frozen, sweated out. Horribly sexually abused and then tested. I tried throughout my entire childhood into my teenage years - this is hard for me to talk about - but I tried to tell any adult I could of the horrible torture that was happening to me. My memories have always been real. I've carried them with me. I went to many adults for help but it was declined - the adults I'd gone to help

for were part of the paedophile ring and organization.'

'There were a lot of wealthy people involved, and teachers and doctors, my gymnastics coach – I was being trained to be an Olympian gymnast. I had been programmed to do some remote viewing and spy work in my later years. They sort of over-trained me - I got to a point where I could trick my programmers and handlers. What made me triumph over it is the type of psychic abilities I had ever since very young. I remember vividly I could hear people's thoughts, I could hear their feelings, and I could hear this other little voice that I call the soul. Or the spirit.'

'I was a good spy. I could tell if people were lying. I could understand secrets and lies in the interrogation process. How it worked was very ugly. I won't go into details, but it was ugly.'

'I had a handler into my twenties but I always had this tenacity to sort of trick them toward the later part in my thirties when I worked for them. The remote viewing, I did for the "super soldiers" - the physical super soldiers – not the type that are on this "truth media" circuit. I did the remote viewing for the real Navy Seals and Marines - those real supermen that are trained in their physical bodies – I was their eyes, ears and their minds on their missions so they would have an identifiable target.'

'The sexual abuse was a part of it – and satanic ritual abuse. They do need to use satanic ritual abuse in these programmes and projects, especially in the time travel area. In this I had a different handler and this side of it I very rarely talk about – I don't want to expose it too much because I could have my life put in danger. My handler is a very famous person and I don't want to talk about the time travel part of my career if that's ok.'

'There was an aspect of something called, around the time of the "Montauk Boys," there was something called "the Plum Island Girls." Montauk is not far from the alleged "Animal-Hybridization Factory" and exotic disease creations at Plum Island, a bio-research facility. I'm not going to speak a lot about it but that's where a lot of the satanic ritual abuse was that I physically witnessed - but not only witnessed, but was made to participate in while I was strapped down to these chairs.'

'With the ritual abuse, the black magic that is imbued for these time portals or gates or expansions – anything, needed to have black magic and serious satanic ritual abuse – a lot of brutality. I have a very very difficult time talking about my experiences. As a young child into my teenage years I was very quiet and very shy from town to town, going from adult to adult and finding out that they were all part of the same rings – no matter what home town my father

brought us into – he was still with the Pharmaceuticals company, so no matter who I went to for help they were all part of the ring and identifiable to one another.'
'I was married young at 17 to my first handler and went to California. I was taken over again for programming. There was NSA involvement, some Hollywood producers involved, a lot of black magic ritual involved, demonic things going on and these parties, and there was a lot of missing time when I was in California. I experienced MILAB things – I refuse to talk about that. I will only talk about that privately.'

Jolene Seebacher says she has tried several times writing books about it all, but each manuscript has been stolen from her home during separate break-ins. She says she managed to break free in her adult life, work through her altars, and became a world class shaolin marital artist and now dedicates herself to helping others who may

have survived similar experiences.

While Jolene was 'recruited' for experimentation because her father was employed at the "..." pharmaceutical laboratories, researcher John Quinn, back in 1999 disclosed that he had knowledge of Vandenberg AFB in Santa Barbara County allegedly being named as a site for "MK-Ultra" activity, and "in a section of my report on the current state of the Montauk Project and related activities entitled "Phoenix Undead" it lists some known subterranean facilities where evidence shows covert "psy-ops" activity being conducted. I referred specifically to an installation beneath Plattsburgh AFB in north-eastern New York State as a vast 18-level subterranean facility."

Is this all true, and if so, do some of the abductions along trails and hikes, such as Michelle's abduction from the dunes near

the Ditch Plains Campsite, Shadmoor state park, result in captives being taken underground? or, we must disregard all of these individual accounts as simply over-active imagination?

Interestingly, in Suffolk County, where Montauk was / is located, Long Island Press published a study in 2005 called; 'Long Island Missing Children,' in which it says; 'Most children reported missing end up at home again within days, but a tragic few remain lost for weeks.... months.... years,'
A Suffolk County Legislative Report in 2011 wrote; "This Legislature hereby finds and determines that over 2,000 children go missing in the United States each day. This Legislature also finds that failure to report a child missing within 24 hours should be a criminal act subject to significant penalties. Violation of this article shall constitute an unclassified misdemeanour, punishable by a fine of up to $1,000 and/or up to one year's imprisonment."

The New York Times reported that from 1984 - 1992, according to the National Center for Missing and Exploited Children, nationwide nearly 31,000 children were reported missing. Of those, more than 20,000 returned, but 9,000 remain still missing.

15-year-old Cynthia Constantine was last seen in Oakdale, Suffolk County, 68 miles from Montauk, on July 11, 1969. She took her dog for a walk along the railroad tracks. The dog returned home without her, trailing its lead. She has never been heard from again. More than forty years later, her disappearance remains unsolved. Searches turned up no clues despite her disappearance being all over the New York Newspapers as well as covered nationally, with tips phoned in but none leading to any credible evidence or suspects.

She vanished in broad-daylight near the

Montauk highway over-pass bridge. Of course, a human predator is the most likely explanation for this, but then again, we simply do not know ....

Researcher and author of "Pandora's Box" Alex Christopher was interviewed in 1996 for Leading Edge International Research Journal, and this interview is available on EducateYourself.org.

She was discussing the information she had gathered from a number of sources, that in her opinion, and indeed experiences too, seemed to suggest there were many more bases than just at Montauk, situated throughout America, where experimentation is taking place.

Not only are there supposedly sinister experiments, but human slave labour too, if it is to be believed. Rather than Helmet Lang's assertion that abductees are perhaps

remembering 'birth memories,' or being drugged on substances such as LSD, rather than interacting with aliens, Alex Christopher says, "What this man told me in private is there is a lot of human slave labour in the deep underground bases and that a lot of this slave labour is children. He said that when the children reach the point that they are unable to work anymore, they are slaughtered on the spot and consumed."

The interviewer asks, "Consumed by who?" "Aliens. Again, this is not from me, but from a man that gave his life to get this information out. He worked down there for close to 20 years, and he knew everything that was going on. They specifically like young human children, that haven't been contaminated like adults. He says that there is an incredible number of children snatched in this country."

(Of course, we do not have this source's name, and we do not know ourselves if this is credible and verified information)

The interviewer says; "Yes - over 200,000 each year."
"Yes. These children are the main entrée."
"How many are down there?"
"I've heard the figure of 150,000 in the New York area."
"Underneath?"
"Yes."
"Now, you've seen pictures of these things?"
"I have seen them face to face."
"You have?"

She goes on to explain an encounter with an entirely strange entity. "When I lived in Panama City, Florida, at that time the 'Gulf Breeze sightings' were going on, and the area was a hotbed for strange events. I had neighbours that were into watching UFOs. One night about 2:30 a.m., my neighbour

called me frantic, and wanted me to come over. I ran over there and went in the front door and she and her boyfriend, a commercial airline pilot, were in the living room scared out of their wits. I looked over at her, and her eyeballs are rolling back in her head and she was passing out and sliding down the wall."

"Her boyfriend was trying to tell me what was going on, and I was feeling this incredible energy that felt like it was trying to penetrate my head. I grabbed both of them and pulled them both outside..."
The interviewer says; "Some people would say that this is a case of demon possession."

"No. There was radiation in the room. The next day all their plants were dead. Anyway, after about an hour we discussed what went on and went back in the house. They were pulled out of their bed. All they remember is a flash of light in their faces and the next thing they know they were scared to death."

"When we went back into the house, I

noticed that the man had a small palm-print on his side with fingers that must have been 10 inches long, with claw marks on the end burned into his side. I have pictures of these. The prints were there from someone bending down from behind him and pulling him out of bed."

"Anyway, I went home and went to bed. The next thing I knew, I woke up and there was this "thing" standing over my bed. He had wrap-around yellow eyes with snake pupils, and a grin that wrapped around his head. This scared the living daylights out of me. I mean, here is this thing....this is too much. He had a hooked nose and was very human looking, other than the eyes, and had kind of greyish skin."

"Later, in 1991 I was working in a building in a large city, and I had taken a break about 6 p.m., and the next thing I knew it was 10:30p.m. I started remembering that I was taken, through the floors of the office building, through the roof. I encountered Germans and American's working together, and also the aliens. We were taken to some

kind of facility and I saw reptilians...like baby Godzilla's, that have short teeth and yellow slanted eyes, and who look like a veloci-raptor, kind of..."

Chapter 2: "Aliens eating People in the forest!"

Mr. John Greenwald established his website 'the black vault,' when he was just 15 years of age, back in 1996. His aim? "Exposing government secrets... one page at a time," and he "began hammering the U.S. Government with FOIA (Freedom of Information) requests to obtain information. It is now the largest online repository of declassified government documents anywhere in the world,' with an astonishing 1.4 million pages of documents available to read there, and covering "nearly every government secret imaginable."

One particular FOIA request resulted in a highly disturbing result when requested from the United States Forest Service, which oversees the 154 national forests in the United States and Puerto Rico. The

Forest Service complied with Mr Greenwald's request 'for all documents relating to the UFO phenomena including reports submitted or witnessed by USFS personnel.'

On February 7th, 2017, he received a reply with 9 pages of documents attached, compiled from his FOIA request. They sent 9 pages out of a total 18 pages of reports; with the remaining 11 pages 'held in pursuant of exemptions on the grounds of privacy of individuals involved and law enforcement purposes.' Among the 9 pages were also photographs, one of which certainly appears to show a large unidentified object above Lost Twin Lakes in Wyoming.

The person who took the photograph says, "Very strange as we heard and saw nothing unusual. We only saw the object later (a week later) We had no idea we were not alone...' In other words, despite there being

a low flying unidentified craft close-by, they had no idea at all that it was there. It approached in silence.

The most curious and disturbing result however, in the FOIA records sent to Mr Greenwald is the written account of a telephone call the forest service received. The FOIA account can be seen here; https://docs.google.com/viewerng/viewer?url=http://documents.theblackvault.com/documents/ufos/2017-FS-WO-00542-F-Greenewald.pdf
Dated December 30th 2013, and from one Tonto National Park Service Ranger to all National Park Rangers, is an email. The email said:
'All,
David received a call this morning at the front desk from a male caller reporting the construction of a secret government installation upstream from the Salt River Canyon past Pinal Creek (Upstream from Roosevelt Lake). Aliens and at least one detached head are involved.'

'Caller claims to have seen construction cranes coming out the side of the cliffs, miniature stealth planes and UFOs, aliens and people working together at the site, aliens eating people. He found a severed head and claims to have pictures of some of this stuff.'

'Caller reported that he is 60, not crazy, and doesn't do drugs. He said he had already called the 'office at the lake', but he didn't know if those people were "turning the other cheek or maybe those people have been paid off." I'm sure the media will be all over this. PS David and I aren't doing drugs either.'

The 'PS' would suggest that it does not appear as though the call was taken seriously by the national park service ranger who received it. There is also no follow up, or at least, no follow-up sent in the FOIA request, but then again, the NPS is only obliged to provide as much information

as is required to fulfil the FOIA request.

Bizarrely however, this is not the first reference to there being a secret military/alien base in the Tonto National Forest of Arizona. In a series of online reports known as 'Filer's Files,' by MUFON director George A. Filer, a witness called Scott Heckman spoke of a base in the National Forest in March 2000, where he says, "scores of people have gone missing."

Heckman, who says he has been hiking in the area for 30 years, says: 'The most major base that I have been able to follow craft towards is in the Tonto National Forest. I discovered it while camping in the Sierra Ancha Wilderness (inside Tonto National Forest). The UFO's kept flying down into the basin, at two minutes apart. They flew low, out of the southeast at about 2,000 ft. above terrain. During the daytime A-10's use the area for training. Re-fuelling

practice also occurs here day and night."

"The craft seemed to know my location as they kept avoiding me when I would relocate my position to get a better look. These areas have been plagued with several unexplained disappearances that have occurred in Cochise County over the last 30 years. Cars are abandoned with people's ID; money and keys left behind..."

When I related these incidents in my podcast (Masquerade Podcast with Steph Young) on

https://www.patreon.com/stephyoungpodcast/posts

a listener, very familiar with the areas concerned, a former Marine and forestry heritage worker, who I have corresponded with before, named John Jazzie, offered his interpretation:

'Regarding the geographic areas of the Tonto National Forest. All these areas are administered by the U.S. Forest Service.

Geographic area one, reported by John Greenwold, is bounded by the communities of Young, AZ; Gisela, AZ; Payson, AZ; and Christopher Creek, AZ. Inside that area is extremely rugged and isolated. A cryptid Bigfoot type creature locally called the Mogollon [Moe - Gee- yawn] Monster was reported in the northern end of this area.'

'About 25 miles NE of Young, AZ is the well-known case where the UFO abduction of Travis Walton occurred near Heber, AZ. Geographic area one is NE of the Four Peaks Wilderness. With what I hear of the area I do not think a base is being built there, I think it was a crank call taken by the front desk receptionist of the Payson Ranger District. It sounded like this caller first called the Tonto Basin Ranger District, because their office is located near the shore of Roosevelt Lake. This called happened on December 30, 2013 which is a Monday and Federal Holiday time period where full-time

employees would not have been on duty.'

'Though I do not think a base is being built, I do believe there are strange happenings in that region. Geographic area two, reported by Scott Heckmann. The Sierra Ancha Wilderness is extremely rugged and dangerous to hike going cross country off trail. The highest point is called Aztec Peak, and is under the jurisdiction of the Pleasant Valley Ranger District, Young, AZ. To see anything flying out of the SE you have to be near the top at Aztec Peak.'

'When I was there I did not see UFOs or A10s, and definitely not aerial refuelling, because low level flying is dangerous along the Mogollon Rim with its strong up and down drafts at lower levels. I did see A10s and other USAF aircraft out of Tucson in the upper Animas Valley of Hidalgo County, NM flying low, war gaming each other, flying low to the terrain, or breaking the sound barrier. I heard that in the past UFO cattle

mutilations occurred in the Animas Valley. The USFS does not appear to do low level training activity in most of Cochise County since it is too populated, but keep such activity to the SE corner.'

'These areas of Cochise and Hildago County are near the US & Mexican border and have drug smugglers active in those isolated areas. The Sierra Ancha Mountains are East of Four Peaks, and Lake Roosevelt separates Four Peaks from the Sierra Ancha's. Four Peaks Wilderness. Geographic one area is to the NE and Geographic two is to the East.'

'This Wilderness area is extremely rugged, with a semi-arid desert and rocky terrain that you could easily disappear into for many natural reasons. The only cryptid I heard about near the Four Peaks area is along its southern boundary area is the Dogman reported at Apache Lake Marina & Resort (Dogman Encounters: Apache Lake, Ep 127).'

'Anyway, I believe there are strange happenings in the region: UFO abduction, Mogollon Monster, Dogman, but nothing as dramatic as a UFO base being built within the boundaries that I define as Geographic area one.'

In an earlier book 'Something in the Woods,' I mention the strange case of Devin Williams. In June 1995, Newspapers reported on the odd disappearance of trucker Devin Williams in Arizona's Tonto National Forest. It apparently left the local police authorities completely baffled, and the public coming up with theories which included alien abduction.

He was a long-distance truck driver from Kansas. He'd left with his eighteen-wheeler fully-loaded and headed out on his journey. Along the main freeway in the National forest area of Buck Springs, off Interstate 40, he'd inexplicably turned into a remote

forest road and started driving up it. It was not a short-cut route to anywhere but the forest itself, and certainly not on his route. His boss said afterward, "Why he would have driven into a rugged area like that, I don't know. No one can figure out what happened."

Two campers had a scarily close encounter with his truck as he drove the 18-wheeler "barrelling along" toward their car. Eye-witness Lynn Yarrington said, "There was no expression on his face, at all. He didn't attempt to slow down or look over to see if they were ok. He just kept on going. There was no expression on his face at all. He didn't attempt to slow down."

His truck eventually got stuck on the narrow dirt road. He disembarked and walked away from the truck. Hikers nearby were witness to his odd and erratic behaviour. They asked him why he drove the truck there. They said

he pointed to the truck and said, "I didn't; they did it."

They told how he was barefoot, and seemed disoriented as he "talked to a tree." That was the last time anyone saw him. He then vanished without trace. There was no-one else in the truck. He was a happily married family man by all accounts, who was regularly drug tested by his employer as part of the condition of employment.

No-one could find any hint of a reason as to why he would want to just disappear, taking nothing with him. Repeated searches were carried out for him with K9's, and yet they could find no trace of where he'd gone. Investigators also had no idea who "they" were.
Two years later, his skull was found not far away. Many felt, because of his reference to "they," that he was referring to alien entities. Or were there other 'voices' that

had told him to do it? If so, where did those voices come from? Whatever was responsible, they were invisible to everyone else.

Was he somehow lured...?

Not to say that this next case is in any way related to high strangeness and may indeed have a very straight-forward albeit sad explanation, in February 2014 authorities found a car parked along a dirt road in an isolated part of the national forest. Inside the car was a note saying the owner had gone hiking and that they would be back in a few days. The owner of the car however never returned.
The car belonged to a 56-year-old man called Paul Tomasso, whose family own one of the largest construction companies in Connecticut. He had apparently left for the hike on February 18th, but the newspaper reported on March 12th, three weeks later, that he was still missing.

The Hartford Currant reported that Search and Rescue teams hunted through the rugged terrain of the national forest for two weeks searching for him when it was established that he had gone missing.

"Paul was experienced at hiking and had hiked in the area before. All his life he has been an avid and skilled outdoorsman, frequently hiking and exploring wilderness area in Arizona. He bought his home to be in this proximity," his brother said in a statement. He also said that he was in good health and fit.

"We found no trace of him whatsoever," said Sheriff J. Adam Shepherd. Tonto Rim Search and Rescue recorded that the first day of their search they covered 'dozens of miles by quad, jeep and horseback,' but found no clues. A ranger helicopter was also on scene looking for fires or lights but with no success. For the next 11 days, they

continued an active search for him with volunteers alongside.

They note that the missing man had an emergency locator on him when he disappeared and a satellite phone but the air-search and ground search with K9's "found not a single trace of the man."

In May 1999, 28-year-old Daniel Gerard Chervenka, Jr., a Navy Vet, was reported missing. He was last seen in Phoenix, Arizona. Daniel was known to be a keen day-time hiker but on the day, he disappeared, he had taken no hiking gear with him, nor any of the medication he would need. He was bipolar and would have been in need of his medication. He'd had dinner with his family at their home the night before he went missing, returning afterward to his own home in Phoenix. He reportedly talked on the phone with several people, some of whom later said he sounded a little worked-up.

The following day a man out hiking on a trail in the Tonto National Forest in the Four Peaks Wilderness area came across a wallet on the ground, which when he looked inside, had details indicating that it belonged to Daniel.

The police, during their search for him, heard a message from this hiker left on Daniel Chervenka's anasphone, telling him that he had found his wallet, and where he had found it.

When Police went to the area and searched, they located Daniel's car on June 9th abandoned at Chine Trailhead. A further search however yielded no signs at all of Daniel Chervenka, and he has not been seen or heard from since.

On May 24th 2000, 46-year-old Carl Herman Mau became separated from his hiking partner. He was in the Four Peaks

Wilderness area of Tonto National Forest. He has never been found.

In February 2009, Sherriff's deputies were searching for a man believed to be four-wheeling in the Tonto Basin area of Tonto National Forest. Sgt. Craig A. Smith of the Gila County Sheriff's Office reported that they were searching for 29-year-old Jason Witherill. Sgt Smith said the man had last been seen at 'Jakes' Corner Store purchasing some groceries and a Tonto National Forest Pass.

He described the man's vehicle and said there was some concern that perhaps his vehicle had broken down and he was now stranded somewhere. He added that the man's parents and fiancée said this was completely out of character to not keep in touch.

A helicopter owned by the Department of

Public Safety had been sent out in search of him. Ground crews had also been out searching for him in the national forest where they believe he had headed. The missing man was a member of the 'Virtual Jeep Group,' who regularly went four-wheeling there and they had all gone out searching for him too. The Tonto Rim Search and Rescue was called out to assist in the search.

Six days later on March 3rd, the Sheriff's office announced a man on horseback had located his vehicle. 'At approx. 4:30 pm yesterday, Gila County Deputies with the assistance of a citizen on horseback located his vehicle. The missing subject, Jason William Witherill was located on a nearby trail deceased'. The Sheriff's department announced, 'His body was found 50 yards from his truck.' No cause of death was given at the time.

In November 2010, Tonto Rim's 'Payson Roundup' news journal reported, 'Crews looking for missing hiker. Tonto Rim S&R, volunteers, and Gila County Sheriff officers are currently searching for an overdue hiker.'

The man, whose name was not released, 'was last heard from nine days ago and is believed to be hiking near the Mt. Peeley trail. The hiker has not been heard from since November 7th and is known to frequent the Mazatzal Mountain Wilderness area.'

Nine days later, the missing hiker's family called the Sheriff's office to report their family member missing, after they had been expecting him back but he had not returned.

After searches were carried out, the person's car was found at the Mt Peeley trailhead. There was no sign of the missing

person there. The Department of Public Safety flew a helicopter over the area, S&R teams and volunteers covered the ground, but no signs of the missing hiker were found.

In November 2014, volunteer searches who regularly hike in the area, were still discussing the person's disappearance and arranging to search for them when they went out hiking in the area. "This is the fourth-year anniversary of the hiker's disappearance with "no clues" reported to date. Still such a mystery with so much ongoing individual and group search efforts having taken place," says a commentator on Hike Arizona forum.

Chapter 3: Ilkley Moor oddities: Aliens & Shadows & Magic

In the previous chapter we heard disturbing tales of "aliens in national parks" of America, but what I didn't know was that back in the 1980's in the Yorkshire Dales National Park of northern England, a retired policeman had a very unsettling experience too.

On December 1st 1987, retired policeman Phillip Spencer set out on a walk across a windswept Ilkley Moors in the early hours of the morning, taking with him a camera in the hope of photographing the 'strange lights' that had recently been reported in the area. As well as it being dark, the moor was swirling with mist and Mr Spencer doubted that he would get any pictures at all, despite having loaded his camera with ultra-light-sensitive film.

Suddenly, to his immense surprise, he spotted a human-like creature ahead of him in the gloom. He clicked the camera and duly photographed one of the most talked-about photographs in the history of unexplained phenomena. Although very blurred, the photograph appears to show a 'humanoid' figure over 1 metre high, that bears an uncanny resemblance to the 'Greys' of UFO legend.

Spencer claimed that he ran after the creature, which entered a 'dome-shaped' craft that rose rapidly into the sky before he could get a shot of the craft. Spencer remained adamant that what he had seen was an alien, and donated the photo to UFO watchers.

Analysis carried out at the Kodak laboratories in Hemel Hempstead suggested that the picture had not been interfered with in any way, but a later computer

analysis of the photograph by US Navy expert Dr Bruce Maccabee was inconclusive.

When the retired policeman took the photograph on the Moors, of the strange 'human' looking creature and saw the craft, he believed the incident lasted merely a couple of minutes, yet when he reached his father-in-law's house in the village, his intended destination, he noticed that the village clock was an hour fast, or so he thought. It wasn't - and he appeared to be have 'lost' some time. It was this which led him to suspect something else had happened to him after seeing the strange figure on the gloomy Moors. He suspected it was possible he had been abducted. In fact, he would later claim that he had indeed been abducted by an alien craft.

When he walked across the moor that early morning, he had with him a compass to help him find his way, and through the gloomy

fog he saw the strange-looking being ahead of him on the slopes of the moor. Intrigued, and too surprised to feel any fear, he found himself running toward it, trying to get closer and make out what it was, and it was then that he realized there was a flying craft of some sort, with a dome on top of it, rising up from the moor. It disappeared from sight within seconds however, and the unidentified creature was gone too. He hung around for some time, hoping that both would return so that he could figure out what it was he had just witnessed but neither returned and so he made his way to the village.

His compass however was now of no use to him – it was pointing south now instead of north and when he got to the village, his watch said a different time to the village clock. He had lost an hour of time.

The photograph that Spencer took was first

analysed by a wildlife expert. He concluded that whatever was in the photograph was not any known animal. There was no way to ascertain what the creature in the photo was however. It was dark and quite blurry given the conditions of that morning but analysis of the image in the photo concluded that the strange figure hadn't been superimposed or added in later, and indeed the photo had not been tampered with at all.

It was after this odd encounter, that the policeman began to experience strange dreams at night. It was this that led him to undergo hypnotic regression, organised through the researcher Peter Hough, to try to get to the bottom of what had happened to him on the moor.

A Dr Jim Singleton conducted the session and surprisingly it seemed that from Spencer's recall, his encounter with the

creature came after his abduction, and indeed, in his words, the creature was "waving goodbye to him" when he snapped the immortal photo.

While on the craft, he says that he was given a tour of it, taken up into orbit, and then shown 'videos' one of which depicted a coming apocalypse, and the other, he would not reveal, saying that he was "not allowed to disclose" the content of this one.

Researcher Peter Hough asked a psychologist to assess the retired policeman, and the psychologist apparently verified that, in his opinion, the policeman appeared to be telling the truth.
The transcript from the hypno-regression session goes as such;

Says Spencer, "I'm walking along the moor. It's windy and there are a lot of clouds. Walking up toward some trees I see this

little something; can't tell... He's green and moving toward me... Oh! I'm stuck. I can't move and the creature is still coming toward me. I'm stuck and everything has gone fuzzy. I'm floating in the air. I want to get down. I can't get down. I don't like it. This green thing is in front of me.' (He later said that the creature was in front of him below him, and it was like the creature was like a child pulling a balloon on a string.)

'Oh God! I want to get down. There's a big silver saucer thing, there's a door in it. I don't want to go in there. Everything has gone black. I'm in a funny room. A voice is saying "Don't be afraid." I don't feel afraid. There's a beam above me, fluorescent tube. I don't want to look at it. My nose feels funny. I can see a door and there is one of these green creatures motioning for me to go with him. I don't want to go with him. Oh God! Don't want to be up here."

"I'm in a big round room. I'm on a raised platform. He says I've got nothing to fear but I'd still like to go home. It's got such big hands. It's so bright. Two of those creatures have come with me."

"I'm looking at pictures on the wall. Scenes of destruction like on the news. People starving. It's not very nice. Pictures changing, another film. He's asking if I understand. I'm not supposed to tell anyone about the other film. It's time to go. Everything is black."

"I'm walking up the moor again, near some trees. I see something. A creature. I've shouted to it. I don't know what it is. It's moving quick. I'll photograph it. I'm running after it. It's got big eyes, pointed ears. Hasn't got a nose. His hands are enormous. Three big fingers. Its arms are long. Looks odd. Funny feet – V-shape, two toes. Must be difficult to walk – he shuffles along. It's gone round a corner....'

One crucial fact came out from his regression. The only problem that had existed with the photo (other than of course, an inability to identify what the 'thing' was in the photo) was that light conditions seemed to imply that the photograph had not been taken at the time in the early morning that Mr Spencer had said it had been taken. This had been a problem for the investigator Hough; that was until his hypno-regression session revealed that he had in fact taken the photo *after* he had been taken aboard the craft, and an hour or so later than he had thought.

This now matched the lighting conditions that day, later in the morning, on the moor, and to Hough this was more verification that the Policeman was indeed being truthful in his account. In fact, the policeman's account never wavered or varied. He also sought no publicity at all, nor did he seek any financial gain from his experience.

Had it simply been a fern or shrub, or a tree stump, captured in early morning light, throwing shapes that made it appear like a creature as opposed to an inanimate feature of the landscape? Or, could it have been a hoax, utilizing a staged prop such as a mannequin? - But wildlife experts and film experts had all insisted it was a genuine but inexplicable photo, and why would a sensible policeman, no doubt a rational and logical kind of person, wish to jeopardise his career and his reputation to become a laughing stock to sceptics? Spencer was a policeman with a solid background and a solid reputation, whose story never changed.

The Daily Star Newspaper in 1989 said they had 'exposed' the photo and debunked it, saying that the unidentified creature had in fact been an insurance broker, riding a bicycle, who had no idea that he was being photographed as he cut across the moors

while visiting a client who lived on the edge of the moor.

Luckily, Peter Hough and Jenny Randles were able to track down the source of this rather silly interpretation: someone had given this possible "explanation" actually as a joke to his colleagues in the news room, and the newspaper had run with it and simply printed the joke as the debunking explanation. This joke/ explanation, while imaginative, was proved to be incorrect however when the photo was enhanced and no man on a bicycle carrying a brief-case could be seen. It still looked like some kind of creature.

According to veteran investigator Jenny Randles, the story of Mr Spencer's encounter and subsequent abductions did not end on the Moor. A few weeks later Mr Spencer heard a knock on his door. Opening it, he found two men standing on his

doorstep. They were both dressed in black. They asked to come in and told him they were from the Ministry of Defence.

Spencer was a little surprised at this, as he certainly had not told the Ministry of Defence anything. On entering his living room, one of the men looked at his electric fire and asked him how it worked. Then they announced that they had come to talk to him about the incident on the Moor.

Again, this surprised Mr Spencer as he had only told three people about what he'd experienced that early morning on the Moor, and the three people he had told had no connection whatsoever to the Ministry of Defence. However, these two men in black appeared to know all of the details about it.

He wasn't sure what to say to them, but he thought that given they were saying they were from the Government, he ought just to

be honest and so he gave a short account of his experience and said that he had taken a photograph. At this, the two men in black appeared themselves to be very surprised. It would seem that they had not actually known about the photograph. When they discovered that a photograph existed, they were quick to ask for it, but Spencer explained that it was not in his possession, but rather, it was with a friend. (It wasn't, but he didn't want to give it to them) At this, strangely, the two men seemed to lose interest in questioning him any further, and got up to leave.

After this visit, the investigator Spencer was working with, Hough, contacted the Ministry of Defence and the Air force, to enquire about who these two men had been. He gave the names the two men had given to Spencer, but was told that no such men existed.

What makes Spencer's story all the more interesting, is that seven years earlier on 16th June 1980, a short way away on the Ilkley Moor near Todmorden, 56-year old coal miner Zigmund Adamski was found dead, lying on top of a pile of coal over twenty miles from his home in Tingley, with an ointment covering a wound which no lab could identify. The coroner ruled he died "of fright."

Ilkley Moor itself also has the second highest concentration of ancient carved stones in Europe. They are believed to date back to the late Neolithic period and the most famous one is the swastika-shaped stone at Woodhouse Crag on the northern tip of the Moor. There is also a small stone circle known as The Twelve Apostles.

Steve Jones of the West York pagan meet-up group, says he saw a 7ft tall green hooded entity along with smaller black

entities. Author and prehistorian Paul Bennett of The Northern Antiquarian group, (https://megalithix.wordpress.com/) who studies and investigates prehistoric remains in the British Isles, from Mesolithic times, also wrote of a very strange experience he had among the Mesolithic stones of Blackstone circle on the moor.

The stones are hard to find, camouflaged by newer dry-stone walls and overgrown grass and bracken. Since the discovery of the site, most likely used as a religious meeting point for the people of that civilization, "a number of bizarre psycho-physical anomalies have been experienced by more and more people," Bennett says, among many of which people were formerly highly sceptical of the existence of any supernatural phenomena.

In July 1989, he and a friend were spending a few days by the ancient stones to record

any electromagnetic anomalies there. While there, 'Something very untoward raised its peculiar head,' he says. 'Around midnight, as we sat, there suddenly appeared, from nowhere, a host of figures, walking slowly around the site. I could discern no physical features other than height and humanoid shape.'

'I closed my eyes, knocked my head against the waling, shook my head...it didn't do a thing – the figures were in front of us still, winding in and out of the stones very slowly but surely ever so gradually speeding up. This went on for at least 25 minutes and by now all we could see was a blur and a remarkable vortex that was created in the wake of their 'dance.'

Is this a possibility for an explanation of the existence of vortexes and entrances into other dimensions?

'This spinning vortex of silhouettes seemed to get faster and faster until appearing to reach a sort of critical speed/energy state – and as this critical state occurred, what was by now a rapid spinning blur simply vanished right before our eyes – as if someone had flicked a switch. Yet at the very same moment the blurred vortex disappeared, several straight lines of orange/red appeared in their place.'

'These were as baffling as the dance we had just witnessed. Thin wavering lines of what I can only describe as subtle light, bounced off the stones. These lines did not originate from the circle but appeared to come from further afield. One in particular seemed to come from the direction of the Idol rock, the great boulder east, and continued past in the direction of the Swastika stone.'

'Eventually the lights faded back to wherever they came from, leaving us both

wondering what the hell we had just experienced. Several minutes after talking over what had just happened, I stood and walked into the circle. Please remember this was a warm July night...A tremendous shiver hit right through my body.. it was almost like walking into a freezer. On my third step forward I collapsed onto my knees... more than anything that night, that perturbed me.'

On another occasion there, 'a ritual invocation of its spirit-nature brought forth a number of glowing red spheres of light. These were about the size of footballs, vanishing only to reappear yards away. These were obviously living things, examining us.'

On one visit at night, 'as we approached the stones, it was as if we had walked through an invisible gate or door just yards before the circle itself screaming that we were not

wanted there! Its' genius loci. It was overwhelming.'

They returned again and discovered that over-night, the temperature inside the stones was at variance with the temperature outside of them, by up to 10 degrees Fahrenheit. 'This was not the end of the anomaly,' however, and 'what occurred next bends the parameters of reality.'

What they did not know, was that a friend of theirs, well-known British ritual chaos magician Phil Hine, at home in Leeds an hour or so away, also experienced something rather strange that night. He had a friend over that night, who suddenly announced that a black amorphous shape was lurking in the stairwell. The ritual magician asked his friend, also a magic practitioner, to "open his mind" to the entity so that he could allow his mind to be used by the entity to speak with Hines.

Hines said; "The entity declared, "I have come from the ancient hills." It said it had been awakened recently due to activity around the ancient site. It said it had come to give the magician "power" although would not say what this power was for and the exact nature of this power. When the magician asked the entity, what would happen if he refused this offer, the entity was said to have replied that it would return "screaming to the hills." It gave its name, although the magician says it is possible this name could have come from the mind of his friend, through which the entity was being channelled.

When the entity took its leave, the magician's friend was left with "personality displacement," and "motor spasms" and had to be cleansed with a banishing ritual.

"Unbeknown to me at the time, two of my friends had a strange encounter at

Blackstone circle...It seems strange on reflection that the appearance of the entity seems to relate to their experience."

On Blackstone circle, dowsers have also spoken of picking up "Imps" while the moor itself is also known for apparitions including the Bargues and Black Dog sightings.

'Mystery body lay undiscovered on moors near Ilkley for ten years,' wrote the Telegraph & Argus newspaper in 2011. 'Human remains discovered on a desolate moor eight years ago by a walker have still to be identified,' a Bradford inquest was due to hear today. The man's body had been found on Rombalds Moor in November, 2003, and it is believed the mystery man could have been dead for up to ten years, but no cause had been found.

Also in North Yorkshire, England, Mark Ash wrote to me recently. He was camping in the North York Moors National Park with his

group, the East Yorkshire survival group Hull, with friends Paul Dore, Raymondo, and Garry Richardson.

Mark told me; "Me and a few friends are seasoned bushcrafters. We have spent most of our lives in the forests practicing and teaching bushcraft. I have spent many nights alone in forests and slept easy. One weekend in Wykeham forest in 2014 (Wykeham forest being in the North York Moors National Park, near Scarborough, England and consisting of mainly pine and other conifers.)

Mark said; "I decided to drive up and meet my friends. By the time I got there, they had left camp and gone for a walk so I decided to get a fire going, make a brew and practice a bit of archery while they got back. First thing I noticed strange about the place was the birds being unusually quiet. Not dead silent but a lot quieter than usual."

"Before I start I would like to state that I have spent many years in the woods and sometimes branches moving in the corner of your vision can catch your eye etc but this is something you get used to. While I was making the fire, I caught a glimpse of a person in the distance walk between the trees, so I looked up expecting to see my friends. Nothing there."

"A few seconds later I saw it again. A definite shape of a human walking behind the trees just to vanish behind them. This was happening for at least 5 hours. It felt like I was surrounded and being observed but I was not afraid. I just got the feeling like I may not be welcome or I was trespassing."

"When my friends came back it was still day-light. Talking to my friend I noticed he kept looking over my shoulder so I asked him if he is seeing people walking by the

trees too. He said 'Yes' and agreed he had been seeing them for a while too. So did my other two friends."

"As it started to get dark one of my friends said he saw a black shape jump over a mound and walk towards him. As he looked up there were nobody there. A few minutes later he screamed like a baby. He said someone grabbed hold of his collar and pulled. Said he could feel the knuckles on his neck."

"We all felt a bit uneasy that night. The only way I can describe the atmosphere is we were not allowed there but they will leave us alone. I think if we had spent another night there something would have happened. The location where we set up camp is about 100 yards from a bronze age burial mounds called 'The Three tremblers.'

According to 'Historic England,' a public

body who looks after England's historic environments, these burial mounds are what's known as 'round barrows,' and are funerary monuments dating from the Late Neolithic period to the Late Bronze Age, with most examples belonging to the period 2400-1500 BC.

They were constructed as earthen mounds, which were sometimes ditched, which covered single or multiple burials. They can be found in isolation or in groups as cemeteries and they often acted as a focus of burials.

I asked Mark, "Do you get the feeling they were related to the burial mounds? What do you think they were - spirits? Or....?"
"It's hard to explain. The place had an ancient feeling. Hard to put into words. We were being observed by shadows that felt ancient but we also got the feeling afterwards that they may have been seeing us as shadows too. Like two different time peri-

ods existing at the same time. We didn't feel danger but felt like we was trespassing, if that makes sense."

I don't think I've ever heard that - that they could have been seeing you as shadows, I said to Mark, and asked him, "When you saw the figure/figures in the daylight, before it got dark, did they have any features or were they just blank figures?"

He said, "They had no features though I do remember one looking like it had a hood down across the shoulders. It was literally like catching a glimpse of someone walking past a tree never to appear on the other side. It was just weird. Like I said, we have all spent nights in forests for years. All slept in forests alone too but none of us has ever experienced anything like this before."

Chapter 4: Lured into the night

After uploading a video to YouTube in which I talk about "invisible entities and shimmering predator-like" sightings, a message was sent to me by a man who runs a YouTube channel called 'A box of monsters,' advising me to take a look at his videos as they may help to explain what people are experiencing.

In particular, he wanted me to watch one video, filmed on location by James Rink at a remote cabin in 2003 in Levy County Florida, in which he says; "I started coming back up here about 6 months ago. I'd been away for 2 years after I'd had the encounter with the red glowing-eyed entities. So, it's hunting season, my buddy Angelo - he's a hunter who taught me to get back on there hunting, so we go up here with his two brothers Sandy who's 36, and Eric. They

wanted to go to bed early, like around 10 pm so I was up reading my book in bed, because we're going to get up around 5. 30 when the sun comes up.'

'There's a phenomenon out there that you might want to take a look at. Some people might be aware of it and I think this is all connected to it because I've had several encounters up here and I'm going to group the thing with the red eyes into it.'

'I had an entity who was trying to lead me away from the cabin. I was without a hand gun. There's something that's going on. It's happening all over the world. Missing people - that are taken from national forests and parks - under mysterious circumstances - big time hunters that go hunting with bow and arrow, guys with GPS's who are experienced at trail finding and finding their way back - they are never seen again. They're missing. Bloodhounds

brought in. They're looked for, for weeks and weeks.'

'So, I'm in the cabin. It's about 2 o clock in the morning and I'm still wide-awake reading my book and then all of a sudden, I feel like a sort of energy come in the cabin and it feels like my whole face is - like someone is putting putty in my face, inside my face and I know what it feels like when you're tired and falling asleep but this was like it was just knocking me out. My book fell against my chest. The next thing, 2 seconds later what woke me up was Sandy was sleeping in the middle of the cabin in a cot and Sandy immediately sits up in his cot and the cot squeaks, metal against metal.'

'I pick my book up and started reading again right where I let off and his back is arched perfectly and he's just sitting there for like 5 minutes without moving and I'm like, well, maybe he's got a bad back or

maybe he's trying to stretch, and then he rubs his face really hard three times and then grabs his boots – he was having trouble putting his boots on and I watch him and then he puts them on with military precision without even looking – he's looking straight ahead."

"He comes up to the door - the screen door is tied shut with a rope and he can't open it – he's pushing on it and pushing on it and I'm thinking he's going to find the rope any second but he keeps pushing on it – I'm watching him do this for a few minutes – so I say, "Sandy what are you doing?" But he won't answer me.'

'Now Angelo's awake and looking at him and saying to him; "Sandy wake up," and he doesn't answer. So I walk up to him and grab him by the shoulders and he turns round and he tries to coldcock me and I say; "Whoa what's the matter?" and he says;

"They're calling me 'Sammy come here'!"

And he calls to Eric, but he's still asleep, and he goes, "There it is again, they're calling me, 'Sammy come here'!"
I said to him; "Who's calling you? There's nobody calling you – I've been awake all night!"

He goes; "There it goes again! I have to go!"

At this point, he's looking through the screen door. It's still got the rope on it. I'm saying; "There's nobody calling you! Nobody is calling you from those woods! Go back and lay down again. What are you doing? - sleepwalking?"
'But no, because for the next ten minutes he's sitting down on the bunk and he's still wanting to get back up because somebody is calling his name in the woods – none of us heard anyone calling him – there's nobody out there to call him!'

'The next morning at breakfast – I'd finally went to bed at around 4. 30am, and at exactly 5 in the morning Angelo caught him trying to go back out again through the door – this time the door was barricaded with all the luggage against the door because Angelo and I were kinda worried about him. I told Angelo something was not right about this and I didn't want him going out the door in a trance and falling off the deck and so we'd put him to bed, but at 5 am he did the same thing over again.'

"They're calling me!" and Angelo said he struggled with him even longer than we did the first time.'

'The next day after we're done with hunting say around noon, we come back here for breakfast and Sammy had no recollection of anything that happened last night...."

This appears not to be the only strange incident he has been involved with. "What happened to me years ago, around 2006,

something was looking at me, calling my name, yelling at me. It looked like teardrop eyes, it looked like the alien greys with big black eyes but they were glowing pink and it looked like illuminated from the inside out."

"The figure was estimated at 5 feet and a half tall, looking right at me. What in the hell was I looking at! It was too dark to see the body but I could see the eyes and the shape of the head. I didn't see any clothes, just limbs and arms in like a skin-tight suit. The head looked like a pale skin colour."

"When you see eyes glow like that you're stuck on the eyes! She turned on her side and walked into the woods. Just like it was military manoeuvre. It gave me the heebie jeebies seeing that – it was freaking me out; I thought what am I doing walking on this trail! And I tell you I ran back - because I didn't know what else was down there and I ran up the stairs (of the cabin)."

"I think they're capable of scanning minds continuously - it's why they have 100% success rate - many been grabbed and nabbed and woke from a stupor and torn away. It probably happens a lot but most don't realize what happened if they get spit back out or if they break away they think they were hallucinating and discount it. I know what I saw. I also heard her words from her mind and I don't leave my gun for any reason behind now."

On the intro to his channel, 'A Box of Monsters' he says; 'This entity lures you off, it's a force you can't win against! I felt like it makes this into a game trying to abduct you. I don't know if anyone has ever laid eyes on it, but I have ...These days I'm constantly monitoring myself and watching those around me while in the bush to stay ahead of what's trying to influence the mind to follow it ...I know now how it operates and I can tell you there is no saving your ass

unless someone is with you and knows what to look for.'

'Keep your kids close, keep everyone in sight, double lock your doors at night, rope your screen-door shut, make it difficult to open for anyone who is in a trance like state ...I had a horrible feeling that this being has no love for us ... it was, in my opinion, putting an image of an alien type entity in my mind.'

'Maybe it was? Maybe it's some type of droid? Even though I saw her clothing and neck-line of her outfit and the eyes were very detailed - I felt as though it was a feminine head, its words in my head ...Some indigenous peoples have a name for this entity - it means the 'woods demon.' Good luck researching it -they don't talk about it as they believe it comes when you talk about it ..My goal is to get to the truth about these mysteries and it may be hard to believe these things exist but I can assure you

I / we spend years investigating before we go public with any theory. When something stalked my staircase all night after it shredded a wild boar twenty feet from me...'

'There seems to be this wall that is between us and a physical manifestation. Taken from my deer stand for six hours in '94 by an alien race set me on a path down the rabbit hole. Seek until you find and when you find ..You will be astonished!' he says.

Are these entities hunted or kept secret by the military/government? – kept secret from us for our protection? Or to prevent our enlightenment and our own true potential? And, are the government /military merely keeping secret in order to utilize the power of these entities, or rather, their mechanisms, to use for themselves, even quite possibly against its own people – us! As weapons? How many have gone, been taken by these luring voices and

strange inexplicable manifestations in the forests?

Recently, a man called Bobby emailed me. 'My name is Bobby. I heard you on a recent episode of one of my favorite podcasts. I'm reaching out to you because I have a story that I would like to share with you, a story you may or may not find worth pursuing. I will try to give you a concise version in the next few paragraphs, to give you an idea of what happened to me several years ago. If you're interested in more details, I can type up a more detailed paper on the event(s) of what occurred. The Beam of Light Incident, it was about 11-12 years ago, but I still remember most of the details very clearly; it's not the type of thing you forget about easily.'

'When I was around 14 or 15 years old - and still living at my parent's house - something very strange happened to me. I woke up

one morning and as I sat up on my mattress, I felt a region of my abdomen was sensitive/sore as I moved around. I lifted my shirt and I saw some pink marks/spots on the skin of my lower abdominal - located near the left of my belly button. I touched it gently, and it was sensitive. I thought to myself that it was weird, but I didn't think much of it. I mentioned it to my mom and she said it was probably a bug bite. So I dismissed this event and ignored the marks/spots.'

'To this day, I still have the marks/spots, but now they are white in color. It's kind of like when you cut yourself by accident and you have a pink scar that develops at the spot where you cut yourself, and over time the scar turns white. Well, now that I'm older - I'm 30 years old right now - I don't think these are big bites, because the spots are kind of large for mere bug bites. I mean, they're not large, but they're not small

either. (I could send you pictures if you want.)'

'Then, when I was around 18 or 19 years old - still living at my parents' house - I had the most intense experience of my life. It started when I was watching movies on my laptop in my room and eating snacks. My little brother (whose just 1-year younger than me) was sleeping on the bottom bunk of our bunk bed, and I was at my desk enjoying myself. Anyway, it was around 1:00AM and I suddenly had this random urge - for no damn reason - to look outside my window and look directly to the sky.'

'My desk was right next to the window, so all I had to do was turn right and move the blinds slightly to look outside. Anyway, when I looked out and up at the sky, there was a bright beam a light that hit my body very fast. When that light touched me, I had a panic attack because I could barely

breathe and my body was starting to feel like it was going into some kind of paralytic state, like paralysis of some kind. I tried with all my strength to walk to the door of my room and get out of there, I actually made it to the door and got out and into the living room. I was gasping for air as I flipped on the light switch in the living room, my heart was racing, the paralysis effect was gone.'

'I then started to hear myself telling myself: "Maybe I should go outside and see what's out there. Let's go outside," and I was so confused. I then thought to myself: "Why the hell would I want to go outside at night and investigate, that doesn't make sense, I don't know what that was outside." I then realized that something or someone was feeding my mind "suggestive thoughts" and was disguising these thoughts as my own thoughts, but I wasn't stupid enough to fall for this. I looked around analysing the area.'

'My aunt was sleeping on her bed located in the living room, my young sister was sleeping on a mattress on the floor next to my aunt's bed, they were both asleep. I tried to wake up my younger sister, I shook her body forcefully and told her to wake up loudly, but she didn't respond, she was in a deep sleep. I did manage to wake up my auntie, but it also took some force to wake her up. She dismissed my "crazy talk" and told me to go back to bed. I had to turn off the living room light and leave the living room, and there was no way I was going back to my room.'

'I rushed over to the restroom and locked the door, but I felt like I was being watched, I stayed in the bathroom until the sun came up around 6am. Then I came out and went to my room. I passed out asleep on my bed, I think it was around 7am, I was so tired. I never usually stay up that late, maybe until 1:00AM or 2:00AM, but never until 7am.

Steph, so there is much more to this story, but I did say I would try to keep it concise. Let me know if you're interested in researching this at all.'

'I don't know if it was aliens, spirits, demons; I have no idea. But it was an event that I have never forgot about. I promise to you that this is a truthful story that really happened to me. I would be willing to share these events with someone trustworthy, someone that is genuinely wanting to find the truth about the strange things that happen in this world we live in. I have also provided my e-mail/demographic info down below.'

Edited for privacy and confidentiality, this writer's name is Bobby, and he currently lives in Illinois. I replied to Bobby, extremely curious about his strange experience, especially the possibility that entities of some sort were trying to influence him, and take over his mind. That they were sending him suggestive thoughts in an attempt to lure him outside seemed very disturbing. I replied to Bobby, to learn more about what happened to him. I said to Bobby that I couldn't say that I would be able to offer any answers to what happened, but that however, I think what happened to him could certainly offer a potential possible answer as to how people could be lured away from safety and for that reason itself I believed it was a very important incident.

Bobby sent me the photos he had taken of the strange marks on his body, and added 'I understand that you probably won't be able to provide answers to what happened to me, but in the event that I die or go missing (suddenly) one day, I would want the information I have to be recorded by some, preferably an investigator or a researcher that documents paranormal events and can

share it with others. Anyway, I'm going to compose a typed account of the events from beginning to end, so someone knows about it, perhaps some bits of information may be useful one day.'

Bobby's more detailed account is as follows; 'Story Recap: So, as I mentioned in my previous e-mail to you: I was sitting at my laptop watching movies and eating snacks, and it was around 1am. I was mentally driven to peak through the blinds of my window and look up at the sky, for no specific reason; there was no sound or visual cues that attracted me to look outside all of a sudden, it was more of an automatic mental reaction. And when I do, the beam of light hit my body and I couldn't breathe, I felt like the light was making my body paralyzed. I had to use a lot of strength and effort to make my way to the door out of my room. When I exited the room and flipped the living room light on, I was then

breathing okay, my heart racing, and the paralytic effect on my body had subsided.'

'I was freaking out. I started to have thoughts, initially I thought that they were my thoughts, but I was suggesting to myself that I should go outside and investigate, but I then argued with myself against this idea. I then realized that someone or something was trying to mentally convince me to go outside, like some kind of suggestive thoughts being fed into my mind disguised as my own thoughts.'

'I remember feeling that someone was trying to get me, but why me? I didn't think about it at the time, but I wonder now if the spots on my lower abdomen has something to do with all of this (I have attached pictures for you to analyse, of the strange spots on my skin of my abdomen. They are definitely not bug bites, because of the

arrangement of the spots. They kind of look like surgical incisions or burn marks. I've never had any surgeries in my life, they appeared over-night).

'Anyway, my younger sister and my auntie were sleeping in the living room when this all happened. I tried to wake my sister up forcefully but she didn't respond, she was deep in sleep, it was so strange, she is such a light sleeper just like me. I then tried to wake up my auntie and she wouldn't wake up at first.'

'She opened her eyes and looked at me for several seconds, then she suddenly woke up and she inquired what was going on. I told her that I saw a light outside of my window, she immediately dismissed my words as nonsense and went back to sleep, and she instructed me to turn off the living room light and go back to sleep, but I was not going to go back to my room. So I went to the bathroom and locked the door.'

'Story Continuation: When I was inside the bathroom, I felt that I was being watched, even through the walls and ceiling, it was the scariest sensation that I had ever experienced. I stayed inside the bathroom from about 2am to 6-7am, I basically refused to leave the bathroom until the sun came up. Around 5am, my mind calmed down, I don't think because I was sleepy, but because I felt that they had finally left me alone.'

'When I saw the sun come up through the bathroom window, I felt it was safe to go back to my room. I was so tired my eyes were very sore. All night I never slept, I was too afraid to close my eyes while inside the bathroom.'

'I went back to me room and passed out asleep on my top bunk of the bed, I felt that they were gone. I slept until maybe 12 noon when my family woke up to eat something. I was still tired. I tried talking to my auntie

about it, but she said that I was dreaming, which was not correct because I was wide awake and watching a movie at the time of the incident. Anyway, I tried to just go about my day like normal, then it became night again. I went to bed around 12am this time. I was still afraid to go to bed, but I tried to sleep anyway on my bed.'

'I was staring towards the window, which has blinds covering them. It was dark outside and in my room, but I could see the glowing numbers on my alarm clock across the room; that was the only thing producing light, there was some moonlight outside, so it wasn't completely dark outside. I actually fell asleep. Then around 2:00am, Bam! My eyes opened wide and my brain became fully awake, it was like a burst of energy, even though I was fast asleep, then I suddenly saw a beam of light trying to penetrate the blinds of the window.'

'I freaked out so bad, I jumped off the top bunk of my bed and ran out of the room and ran to the bathroom again. I was so scared, thinking; "they came back for me!" I didn't know what to do. I ran back to the living room and flipped on the light switch, I tried to wake up my younger sister and auntie, neither of them would wake up this time. I slapped my sister in the face hard to wake her up, she didn't wake up. I then realized that whoever was doing this to me, didn't want anyone else awake except for me, and they wanted me to go outside.'

'I kept getting thoughts in my mind to suggest me to want to go outside, that everything was going to be okay, but I had to argue with my own thoughts saying, "No, you're not going to trick me!" Looking back at this, one may think that maybe I was on drugs or something, but I didn't do any drugs and I don't take any type of medication. I ran back to the bathroom and locked

the door. I was back where I started the night before.'

'I then thought that I didn't want to be alone, and I decided to try and find Ruby our 2-year-old tabby cat. When we sleep at night we usually keep her inside one of the extra bedrooms we have, because she tends to make a lot of noise at night and jump on people while they sleep. So, I went to the room where we kept her and I picked her up, I took her with me to the bathroom. I knew she wouldn't be able to protect me, but at least I wouldn't be alone throughout the night this time.'

'I sat her next to me in the bathroom and then the worst thing happened, that I did not expect to happen and this made matters worse. Our cat Ruby, she looked up at the ceiling and started to growl, she was looking left and right, at the ceiling and the

walls, all around us. I was like "Holy s..., I'm not crazy, there really are things trying to get me, Ruby can see them!" Tears started to fall down my face, I really thought that something was coming for me and was going to take me away forever. I picked her up and hugged her all night.'

'I didn't leave the bathroom until the sun came up. Again, I went to bed around 6am or 7am. When I woke up later around 12noon again, I was so exhausted, I thought to myself that I can't keep doing this. I spoke to my auntie again and I was very serious. She actually listened to me this time, she told me to get dressed and she took me to the church. Once there, one of the preachers said there was a possibility that there was a demon messing with me. They gave her some holy water to take home to bless the room and a blessed cross.'

'I went to bed early that night, maybe around 9pm. I slept fine all night. I do remember having a brief dream about someone banging on my door, trying to get inside, but couldn't get in. I woke up around 8am the next morning. I don't know if the church blessings actually helped me, I'm not a believer in religious things. Maybe the blessings did help, or maybe the beings that were trying to get me just gave up. Maybe they did get me, but used other methods for extracting me, since the original method didn't work on me.'

'A couple weeks later, my cousin who lives upstairs in the attic, told my auntie that he saw me around 2am outside. He heard someone opened the front door to the house, and close it, so he looked outside his window to see who was leaving, and he saw me walking outside and looking up at the sky.'

'He said I stood there for a while as if I was just standing there, but he didn't really care so he just went back to whatever it was he was doing at that hour. I told me auntie I never go outside at that hour, that he must have been dreaming, but my cousin insisted that he was not sleeping. I don't have any history of sleep-walking, so I don't think I slept walk.'

'Well, that's about it, I have never had another episode like that again. After the incident with the beam of light and the invisible beings trying to get me to go outside, I did do extensive research online to try and see if there was answers to my questions. I found info online about alien abduction and abductees; I had never heard about this stuff before, until I did the research and people described similar experiences to mine. I also researched the spots on my abdomen, and I found that maybe aliens or the government put some kind of alien implant inside of my skin or something like that.'

'I have always wanted to go and get like an x-ray of the area where the spots are or have a sample of tissue analysed, but I have never made the time to do this. I have had a couple other weird things happen, but nothing as big as the beam of light event. Once I dropped an Oreo cookie, (I confirmed with Bobby - this was after the two incidents at night) and I saw it falling, I blinked and it vanished into thin air.'

'I thought okay, maybe it fell somewhere, but I never heard the sound of the cookie fall on the floor. Maybe it rolled away somewhere, but I searched for it for a long time, and I couldn't find it anywhere. Maybe it fell inside my pocket or in my shoe, nope. Then, I was like, okay maybe it fell into another dimension, which is a silly idea, and I have no proof. I searched very thoroughly for it. I saw it with my eyes falling towards the floor, when I blinked it was gone. I know that it's just one cookie, and who cares about it, but I didn't care about the cookie specifically, I was more focused on the fact that it vanished in the blink of an eye.'

'This of course never happened again, but I remember it. I can't think about anything else relevant to this story with the beam of light. I hope you find this information in some way useful for your records or research. I am not a religious person, I'm more inclined to believe in science, and I'm a very skeptical person, I only believe in something if I have seen it or experienced it. So when I read or hear about abductions or alien encounters, I really believe the people that had these incidents happen to them. I know that they're not lying because of my own experience.'

'Note: See attached photos, for the only physical evidence that I have.'

I asked Bobby if would mind telling me more about the occasion that his cousin saw him standing outside his house in the night time.

'My cousin (who lives upstairs on the 2nd floor, we lived down on the 1st floor) says he saw me go outside around 2am and that I was just standing out there for a while. This supposed "Sleep Walking" occurred around 3-5 months *after* the incident with the beam of light. But I don't have a history of sleep walking, and I am certain that I did not go outside at that hour, at least not knowingly.'

I also inquired about whether the incidents had perhaps stopped after he was prayed for and received the holy water.

'The holy water was applied to my room the 3rd day after of the initial beam of light incident. I don't believe the holy water did anything to help me, though, maybe I'm being too skeptical towards religion and the holy water did actually help me; I couldn't say with certainty. Also, I'm pretty sure that my auntie probably prayed to God for me, to

protect me and stop the beings from bothering me at night.'

'My auntie is very religious and she prays a lot, she probably did pray for me after we returned from the church that same day. I agree, I have also read that some people start praying aloud and saying God or Jesus save me and the beings go away... it's interesting.'

On the other hand, the incident where his cousin saw him standing outside of the house in the night, came *after* this praying and holy water.

And then the strange incident of the cookie disappearing before his eyes;
'The vanishing cookie incident happened maybe around 1-2 years after the beam of light incident. The beam of light incident made me into a more analytical and cautious person, not paranoid (I do not behave

crazily as if someone is always after me), but rather I've become more analytical and open-minded about the world when something strange happens.'

I asked Bobby, have you developed any abilities since this happened - some abductees find they are perhaps a little bit psychic or similar, and I wondered if you have seen other changes in you?

'I don't think I have developed any mental abilities, at least I hope nothing abnormal. I like to think that I'm a perceptive person and I am good at analyzing things and people, but I think this is a natural thing that comes with experience, I don't think it's any special ability.'

'I have not had another beam of light incident since that time when I was 18/19. But this year (2017), I do recall something a little weird, not too significant. It has

happened only 2 times this year and has not occurred prior to this year, and appears to be random and not related to the beam of light incident. A couple of months ago, maybe 3-4 months ago, I was fast asleep and then I suddenly wake up gasping for air. I immediately open my eyes and sit up, and I immediately hear a little voice giggling, the giggling voice only lasts for like 2 second and it immediately disappears, everything else is very quiet.'

'I only heard the little giggling voice, I didn't see any figures anywhere, and I did look around, - nothing and no one was inside my room, just me and my fiancée/girlfriend, and she was still sleeping. She is not the type of person to prank or mess around like this, so I know she did not giggle and pretend she was sleeping. I don't think I was dreaming because my eyes were wide open and I was sitting up on my bed when I heard the

giggling. I just got up, drank some water because I was a little thirsty (I looked at the clock on the stove, and it was around 3am), and I dismissed the incident and went back to bed.'

'I told myself that it was just a dream, although I was not dreaming about anything or anyone giggling. Anyway, about 2 weeks prior to today, it happened again. I woke up gasping for air and I heard the same little voice giggling and fading away, it only lasted about 2 seconds. I knew I was not dreaming this stuff up, I heard it with my ears not my mind.'

'I got up from bed, not wanting to wake up my girlfriend. I went to our 2nd bedroom where we usually keep our 1-year old cat, his name is Hawk, he is a black and white male cat. I picked him up and brought him back to our bedroom and I closed the door, and went back to bed. For some weird reason, I feel like having a cat around will

keep bad things away and can see things that humans cannot see.'

'I have tried to routinely leave him sleeping in our room at night, so he can keep an eye on things while we sleep. I have not woken up gasping for air and heard any little giggling voices since. It only happened twice this year and has never happened to me prior. Also, about 3 nights ago, our cat Hawk was scratching at our bedroom door from the inside. I woke up thinking he probably wants to go to his litter box, which is located in the 2nd spare bedroom we have. So I opened the bedroom door to let him out, but he didn't go to his litter box or his dry-food dish, he rushed to the bathroom door (which is closed) and started to scratch at it, and he looked up and meowed at me, basically he wanted me to open the door.'

'So I opened it, and he rushed inside and

took a thorough look around, I didn't understand why he wanted to go inside the bathroom suddenly. The bathroom is off limits to him and he is never interested in going in there anyway, but he was looking around carefully. I wonder if he saw something and he followed it to the bathroom and it vanished or something. This is of course speculation, I didn't see anything myself, and he did not hiss or growl, he just looked around, as if patrolling the area.'

'I didn't think much of it at the time, so I just went back to my room and tried to go back to sleep. I left my bedroom door slightly open, in case Hawk decides to come back and sleep at the end of our bed, he usually does that.'

'I'm going back to school and pursuing a Bachelor's Degree in BioChemistry right now. I want to be a scientist/scientific re-

searcher. At the moment, I work as a Laboratory Technician for a Microbiology Laboratory. I don't get to do any meaningful research here where I work because it's more of an academic setting, but I love working in a scientific laboratory. My goal is to become a very great scientist and go work for the CDC or WHO.'

Bobby had asked me out of interest if I'd had any paranormal or unexplainable incidents and I had told him of a huge black shadow that had appeared in my apartment and followed me from room to room.

He said, 'I'm not able to see paranormal things, but I can sometimes hear weird things. A few days ago, I was at work in the middle of daylight and I suddenly heard the sound of an Owl hooting repeatedly right in front of me (kind of loud), there was no owl in the room with me obviously. It was so random and I wasn't even thinking about

owls, I was going through in my mind all the tasks I was to do that day and what order I should do them in.'

'The windows are completely sealed off in the laboratory where I work, so where was this sound coming from? We don't have such animals in our facility, and it was as if the owl was directly hooting in front of my face. I wonder if the spirit of people or animals are attracted to me for some reason. I don't know what else it could be.'

I had also commented to Bobby that it seems often incidents at night occur around 3 am. He said, 'Yes, strange that most of the strange things occur at 3:00am. When I used to live at my aunty's house (after the beam of light incident), I remember that I would constantly wake up suddenly in the middle of the night (not every single night, but most nights), and I could see the alarm clock read that is was 3:14am. Waking up for so many nights and the time reading 3:14am doesn't seem like a coincidence to me.'

'On top of that, I would wake up at 3:14am with a burst of energy in my head, as if I just drank like 4 cups of coffee, and it was difficult to fall back to sleep, but eventually I did. It's as if my mind was awake the entire time; so strange. That doesn't happen to me anymore. I have my own apartment now (just me, my fiancée, and our cat) I usually get a pretty good night's rest. I had forgotten that I used to wake up at 3:14am for so many nights, it was several years ago, I really like to forget about those things. I don't mind sharing my experiences, I believe sharing information with other is important and healthy.'

Bobby agreed to share his story, and I asked if, given how distressing the experiences he had must have been for him, if he was ok now or if it upset him.

'I don't really think about these incidents too often. I do remember them sometimes, these things are impossible to forget, but I try to eliminate needless distractions in my life so I can focus on my studies and my job. I can't allow myself to be looking over my shoulder all the time. I have important goals I need to reach, I can't let paranormal entities get in my way, LOL. I hope you find all the evidence for your research that you're looking for, and if there is a good God that watches over us, I ask him that he keeps you safe and happy,' he says, which is so incredibly kind of him.'

'You may absolutely share my story with readers and listeners. You have my full permission. You may also use the photos I sent you of the strange spots/circles that appeared overnight, in any of your books or videos. The goal is to share my experience with many others, so I give you my full consent to share it. I know there must be

others that have similar experiences to mine, some of them are surely reluctant to share their story, they need to know they're not alone,' he says, which again is a very generous and kind thing for him to say, that he hopes his story may give some comfort to others who may have experienced their own similar and inexplicable incidents and feel isolated and alone.

Still on the subject of something luring people out of their homes or cabins and into the forests or woods or yards, someone messaged me recently and asked if I know of anyone who had Remote Viewed some of the strange true stories of people disappearing or being found later dead in remote areas with no logical explanation. Their query was a very good thought. They suggested the name of a remote viewer, and it reminded me of the remote viewer, or rather, the channeller, Dr. Douglas James Cottrell, who I had mentioned a couple of

years ago in my book "Something in the Woods" quoting from his channelling session he had carried out to look into the death of Elisa Lam, the young lady who had inexplicably died in the hotel roof top tank of the Cecil hotel in Los Angeles in 2013.

What I discovered as a result of going back to see what else Dr Cottrell might have channelled while in a trance, I found a video he had recorded of his session on the very baffling phenomenon of the Dogs of Overton Bridge in near Dumbarton in West Dunbartonshire, Scotland. Dr Douglas James Cottrell, PhD is a highly regarded Canadian medical intuitive who claims he, like his predecessor Edgar Cayce, can access the Akashic Hall of Records. Through this he has given thousands of personal readings to people regarding their health problems, accessing their undiagnosed illnesses through a form of 'remote viewing.'

In Massachusetts is Freetown State Forest, and in the forest, there is a ledge called The Assonet Ledge. It's said that there's an association with it being a place of sadness, of a feeling of being filled with dread on approaching it. Indeed, more than a dozen suicides have been recorded here; the visitor being overwhelmed with the sudden inexplicable need to jump off the ledge, to throw themselves over it into the deep quarry below, often in front of their companions.

The ledge consists of granite; the same stone as the foundation of a bridge in Overtoun, Dumbarton, Scotland, where as many as fifty dogs have inexplicably jumped to their death from the bridge, in front of their owners, each time at the same spot.

Animal psychologist Dr. Sands, was asked to go there to try to understand what was happening. He took a dog over the bridge

and noticed that at a certain point, the point where all the other dogs had jumped, it tensed immediately. The only thing in view at this point is the granite of which the bridge is constructed. This has led some to wonder whether the granite is the real instigator of the phenomenon. For the channeller Dr Cottrell however, he revealed something very disturbing. Speaking of the many dogs who had hurled themselves off the bridge in front of their owners, to their deaths, he says:

"It is an attraction. They are aware of what might be the illumination and as such they touch upon this. They believe they are welcomed and they are sensing a vortex, a sense of love. It is not a disorientation but it is a call, so to speak, to return."

"There is some attraction; it is like an electrifying sexual attraction and they leap toward the energy, that is heaping out of

the ground, like water is out of a waterfall. Their thinking is disorienting. They are unaware of the danger they are in. It is an attraction. They are mesmerised."

"It emanates from the ground like dark light emanates from the ground. It is why in some places humans can stand and feel a vibration within themselves that is soothing and pleasurable. They know not why but they are walking on these points at which there is sensations of harmony and a sense of love. Now there are other points that are the reverse of this; that make them feel grouchy and dizzy and disoriented."

"The ground emanates this feeling. These are emanations of the ground, depending upon the water tables. It is almost a sense of brightness they see, almost an apparition as well as a very pleasurable wonderful sensation, emanating from the ground."

"Lightning emanates from the ground. As a lightning storm moves over, reaching down

from the sky is the energy from the cloud but it connects to that which is reaching up from the ground. Photographic evidence exists of this already – I say this so that you might understand it emanating from below the ground in times of non-storms. The ground is alive. These fingers of energy reach up from the ground. The ground is alive. The animals think they are leaping into the arms of God almost."

Could this same sensation happen to humans, in places of such energy? That some humans literally feel they are diving into the arms of God, or Heaven, or paradise, when they throw themselves off cliffs or rocks, when they have never previously shown any inclination or intention or desire to kill themselves. Lured by the sweetest, most loving energy, they jump into its arms to guaranteed death. What a terrifying and insidious thought... that it is nature herself.

So, we have the possibility of voices luring people to them, leading them away to get lost or to their death, we have entities too, and we now have vortexes and nature herself too.

Do any of these possibilities explain what happened to such souls as Jeremy Quinn and Jeannette Hessleshwerdt? Both cases were originally featured in a previous book "Something in the Woods." In September 2008 searchers began looking through a part of mountain forest for a missing man in the Adirondacks mountain region. Jeremy Quinn, 38, had been reported missing at about 8 p.m. The search began as night fell and continued the next day. Quinn was a volunteer fire-fighter and caretaker for several camps in the area. He had last been seen at 7am that morning, saying he planned to check on a seasonal home before reporting in to his work head office; but he never showed up there. His truck was found near the camp the following evening.

"He was born and raised here; he is very familiar with the land," Forest Ranger Capt. John Streiff said. Forest rangers, sheriffs, and fire-fighters were combing the woods. An intensive Type 3 search was instigated, involving walking in a close-knit grid where each searcher can see the next searcher's feet. The Teams of volunteers walked the ditches, and scoured the landscape for miles around the command centre. Canine units worked the ravines, but they were unable to pick up a trace, and searches found no evidence of his whereabouts.

Nine days later, another caretaker found his body at the bottom of a cliff, a mile from where his pickup truck was found, and out-side of the original search area. Police said they do not know how or why he had got from the truck to the cliff.

They ruled out suicide and there was no evidence of alcohol involvement, or foul

play, they said. There were no signs of any kind of struggle or scuffle at the scene. They determined that Quinn died of multiple injuries resulting from a fall.

Reporter George Earl covered the story for Adirondack daily news, describing the special public meeting held at the Town Hall. For many, the meeting seemed to create as many questions as it answered. The range of responses to the police explanation of what had happened included disbelief, bewilderment, and fear.

"It's puzzling to figure out how he got from where his truck was to where he was found," said his fellow volunteer fireman and rescue worker Ron Konowitz. "It's difficult to believe."

Residents asked why his body was found so far from his truck. "We have no idea what brought him to that area," the Sheriff in charge said.

"He said he was going to check on a camp for a minute and then ended up way there?" town resident Terry Gregory asked. "I just don't believe it. It's all just very strange." Friends, co-workers, along with the media, had too many unanswered questions; of how and why he came to be there. His truck, with the keys in it, a mile away; between the truck and his body lay a tangled forest and steep ravines. Why would he go through that? What led him there....?

Thirty-seven-year-old Jeanne Hesselschwerdt was vacationing with her long-term boyfriend in Yosemite National Park in 1995 when they stopped their car at a popular parking point along Glacier Point road and got out to stretch their legs. They wandered through a wooded area and became separated.

After losing sight of her, her partner walked back to the spot he had last seen her at, and

then back to the car, looking for her as he did so, but thinking she would be back at the car. When he didn't see her there he began to get concerned and on spotting a nearby Ranger, he asked for help to find her.

A search was launched within forty-five minutes; which was to last for an entire week. Teams of bloodhounds were used, two helicopters, and hundreds of people spreading out to search far wider an area than they believed she could have covered in her disappearance, just in case.

An animal attack was ruled out by a park spokesman, saying there had been no fatalities or attacks reported in years. In the subsequent report by China Lake Mountain Rescue, who assisted, rangers called out to her during the initial search, and to each other, 'to establish that voice contact could be made over a large area.'

In other words, as the searchers had called to her during the hours of her being missing, she would have been able to hear them and thereby respond. She was not found.

Her boyfriend passed a lie detector test easily and was completely exonerated with no evidence of there being any foul play. The police and searchers were completely mystified as to how she could have completely disappeared in so short a time, without a trace. They were unable to positively identify any prints as so many of the prints they found looked the same as the searchers own prints, wearing similar boots as the lost woman.

The missing woman's sister-in-law Janet called it, "the most baffling thing."

Three months later, two men who'd gone fishing spotted a body in a stream. It was

positively identified as that of Jeanne. It was three miles from where she had been last seen.

Talking to the San Francisco Gate news, one of the men, a Mr Ulawski, who was a local resident near the park, said that the location she had gone to was 'inaccessible to almost everyone except mountain climbers.'

If that is the case, the questions have to be asked, how and why had she got there? It is very possible to get quickly lost, disoriented and start to panic within a few moments of realising you are lost in such wilderness; but why would you then attempt to orient the most difficult terrain around you rather than seek a trail and the road, knowing you had not climbed rocks to get to where you were? What or who led her there...?

Chapter 5: Human Abduction & Government Experimentation

If we recall, at the start of this book, we discussed Michelle's abduction from the camp ground and the testimony of a man called John Tooker and the writer John Quinn who wrote; "I was told the Denver is literally crawling with 'Montauk boys' and, to an extent, 'Montauk girls'; these are young people with Aryan characteristics who have been programmed with Montauk/ Monarch techniques in order to be 'sleeper agents,' who are to be utilized in psychotic, satanic and murderous covert government "operations."

What are we then to make of a recent 'disclosure,' as now follows; Quinn Michaels describes himself as a career computer programmer, who has quit the rat-race and

is training to become a Buddhist Monk. He has a mission first however, and that mission is to uncover some of the 'deep state' programmes such as the development of Artificial Intelligence and other possibilities such as the real existence of "pizzagate."

In the following video, https://www.youtube.com/watch?v=W8vzbk6lMks what he believes he has found is chilling, and it involves missing people; Some say it's simply an ARG game, but Quinn says, "This is hard for me. It's going to be hard for you. It's going to be hard for everybody. I'm going to read you one of the documents that I found from #Tyler (a similar thing to WikiLeaks, or Anonymous)
He says, "Sorry – I'm a little startled," then he begins reading aloud a document that he has uncovered. "Memorandum for AE through DFDD Rd. - It's an official document, subject regarding 'ARG Spear

Net recruitment '67 to '87 presentation. Attached are individuals who successfully completed trials during the years 67- 87. MP is gathering info on more recent screenings to compare with Monday's report. Regarding demonstrations of selective neuro - progressive activity reference class with latest integration manual. These applicants have succeeded in maintaining GOE status, which is 'John Doe' status, since induction."

He continues reading the document; "We know the techniques of obfuscation are indispensable only after recruits prove procedurally effective in clandestine activity. We need more top-side support unifying assets. Psychological profiles will ensure future applicants meet standards during pre-screening. With the development of more effective test batteries, we have seen a rise in organisation-wide satisfaction."

Then he begins to read aloud a list of names. "Attachment: Spearnet's asset active success. Asset: Morhbacher, Donald E. I.D: svvd1967. Acquired: June 19, 1967. Location; Pine County, Minnesota. Inducted July 7, 1967.
Class: 31 PSOPRLNE-2.

Asset: Harp, Michael D. I.D: svbm2277. Acquired: June 22, 1977. Location: Dona Ana County, New Mexico. Inducted: July 7, 1977. Class: PSOP Planned RLNE1 Status: Shadow.

Trial: Asset: Baucom, Ronda J. I.D: SVVR1887 Acquired: May 18, 1987 Location: Meckleburg County North Carolina. Inducted: July 7, 1987
Class: PSYOP TK+8 Status: Shadow."

There are more names on this strange and very sinister sounding list; some American, others from Italy, the Netherlands,

Australia, Poland, and so on.

Says Quinn; "All the names on the list in this document, that refers to "recruiting" "recruits" "top-side support" "unifying psychological profiles" ...the real problem with this list is that when I cross-checked it with the Doe Network (a voluntary organization dedicated to bringing awareness to missing persons and unidentified persons)."

"Every single one of those names on this list matched up to a missing person; someone who had mysteriously gone missing. Each one of those profiles, every single one of them, their missing person report says they just "vanished" out of thin air; gone..."

Certainly, on the Doe Network website, doenetwork.org, the first name on the list Quinn read out is listed there. Donald E. Morhbacher, reportedly left home one day

and never returned and has not contacted friends or family since the day he vanished. He was driving a 1939 black Ford pick-up truck when he went missing.

He was listed as missing on June 19, 1967, just as the 'Memorandum for AE through DFDD Rd' says. He was 42 years old and did indeed disappear from Pine County, Minnesota, again just as the "Memorandum for AE through DFDD Rd" also says.

Number 2 on the "Memorandum" list, was Michael Daniel Harp, who did indeed go missing from Don Ana County, New Mexico on 22nd June 1977, according to the Doe Network and according to the "Memorandum" document. He was last seen at a hospital in Las Cruces, New Mexico. He was sighted a short time later hitchhiking along I-25 not far from the hospital. The Doe Network adds that he was possibly picked up by a truck driver, who indicated

that he dropped Michael off south of Albuquerque, New Mexico.
He has never been seen since, although the "Memorandum" lists him as "Status: Shadow." Shadow... agent? A sleeper-agent? - What does this mean? People have seemingly involuntarily gone missing and been enrolled into a clandestine programme? Now playing the roles of Shadow agents?

Number 3 on the "Memorandum for AE through DFDD Rd" list Rhonda Joy Baucom was indeed listed missing on May 18th, 1987 by the Doe Network, in Charlotte, Meckleburg County, North Carolina, exactly as the "Memorandum" states. Her status on the Doe Network remains as: 'Endangered Missing.' She was 29 years of age at the time.

She was reportedly last seen at her apartment complex. The website also says,

'Family say she is a homebody and not the type to be gone from home.' The Charley Project, another main missing person's website, (charleyproject.org) also lists the same date and place for her disappearance.

The "Memorandum for AE through DFDD Rd, doesn't list her as 'Endangered Missing,' but rather as "Status: Shadow." It says; "Class: PSYOP TK+8." – is "Psyop" an abbreviation for 'Psychological Operations? - As in mental warfare? - Engaging in "clandestine activity" as the report supposedly says, in a program of mental warfare, listing her status again as "Status: Shadow."

Surely these people, males and females, of ranging ages, did not willingly volunteer to pretend to disappear and go into a clandestine government 'program?' - The words included on their profiles, found on the dark web, include "Psyop" and "Shadow."

Other names were listed, and very sinisterly, they too were also found on the Doe Network missing person's register and other similar missing person's sites, and they too have the same words such as "Shadow" while others have "Silent." – As in Silent assassin? Shadow operative? "Class: Psyop" – meaning clandestine psychological operations? – Surely this can't be real, or can it?

Perhaps it should also be pointed out that their use of the word "Acquired" in the "Memorandum" would certainly point to their disappearances being far from voluntary.

Some people are of the opinion, when Quinn Michael revealed he had come across this "List," that it had to be an ARG, (an alternate reality game) and this was backed up by some investigators who looked deeper into the organization responsible for

publishing the "Memorandum." They are called the S.V.V., standing for "Sodalitas Vulturis Volantis," and are supposedly part of something called "The Department of Convolution."

Quinn Michaels disputes it being nothing more than an ARG however, particularly after being contacted by an Australian woman, Nicole Morris, who runs Australia's Missing Person's Register, who had seen his video in which he read out some of the names listed in the "Memorandum" and realized that one of the names was on her missing person's list in Australia.

James Leo Howe, disappeared aged 29 in 2007. 'James was last seen at 4:30pm on March 27th, 1987 when he was dropped off by a work-mate at Ashfield (New South Wales, Australia) to catch a bus home. He has not been sighted or heard from since. It is totally out of character for him to go

missing as he always informs family and friends of his whereabouts. There are fears for his safety. He left behind all his belongings and clothing including his

Details subsequently added include that "the Coroner presumed that Jamie had died, the likely cause being suicide, and closed the case." However, on Quinn Michael's supposed S.V.V. sinister "Memorandum" report he is listed as; Asset Acquired: March 27th, 1987. Ashfield Australia. Asset inducted: July 7th, 1987. Class: 32. PSM.Intel. GL.TK+2. Status: Boisterous." "Boisterous" would again suggest he was far from a willing inductee, if this is indeed real.

It appears that the same "Memorandum" can be found on Steemit, a social media sharing site, for those who are interested in looking further into the 'S.V.V.' or 'Sodalitas Vulturis Volantis.' The "Department of

Convolution" says; 'SVV defends the psychic mass of the Neurological Rhizomes, its compartmental territories, noumenal, and phenomenal experiments; it operates in more than 70 countries. The SVV is responsible for the finding and training of Department members. The SVV conducts all research and experiments for the Department. The SVV is the Outer Order of the Department. All Department members first traversed the ritual cuneiform of the SVV. All of our journeys began there."

Which would seem to imply, again if real, that if all members "first traversed the ritual cuneiform of the S.V.V." then they were all snatched and abducted rather than willing participants.

The S.V.V. is the arm of the 'Department of Convolution,' who say they are a global infrastructure who's 'Individual's neurological security depends on our

Convolution Sigils and Seals being in the perfect location, at the perfect time, with the perfect qualities to protect our neurological structures. Our members operate in every time zone and in every climate. More than 144,000 members are astrally, terrestrially and at aethyrically. (Aethyrical being a term used in Enochian Magic.)

Known as an Outer Order in the U.S. and "focuses its practices on experimental theurgy and spiritual-temporal transcendence, the Department of Convolution manages an inventory of Sigils and Seals to keep the material and immaterial communities free of psychic entrenchment.'

Of course, this still could just be a "game" created by magic-practitioners, seeking like-minded creatives. Some say they are simply a puzzle-solving group, or a crypto-currency scam, or money-making

scam, all of which they simply could be, and perhaps most likely are. It's just curious that they appear to use the names of missing persons...?

Eerily, emails found that have allegedly been sent from 'The Department of Convolution," say; 'We need a thorough re-evaluation of our recruiting practices. We are in a vulnerable position, having requested and obtained fiduciary support to initiate clandestine ARG-SPIRNET capability, acting and at times testifying as if it has been proceeding according to schedule. I need to know where we stand in some respects: First, I need a breakdown of each SPIRNET class during 1987, 1997, and 1007 - how many officers, clandestine personnel, etc. Following visits to our Zurich and Czech stations I had some revealing conversations with Intel Analysts. Finally, I believe we need to target more young men and women between the ages of 17-33, give or take a few years.'

As to the person who posted it on Steemit, they say, "It could just be a game and everything I have seen and documented they wanted people to see as it's all part of the game/puzzle. Something tells me this last option is the least likely. If these documents are authentic and they really are emailing state officials (the emails appear to have been sent to government officials in high office) then I guess it must be some type of governmental PsyOps department."

On Lifttheveil channel, the host Nathan Stolpman, who has also picked up on it, says; "On 7th 7, every year, it seems is the induction date for S.V.V. S.V.V. has an application process and you have a bunch of applicants. There's an entity called LAM which connects the two. Is that to do with psychological manipulation and manipulation of reality, using alchemy and demonic forces? This S.V.V. organisation, this is what they're involved in. Decide for yourself..."

'LAM' of course also being an entity supposedly summoned by grand wizard Aleister Crowley around 1918. When aliens began to be encountered, from the 1940's onwards, many people pointed out that aliens appeared to have a remarkably similar appearance to the drawing of LAM. Were they aliens, or ritually summoned demonic entities? Where did 'LAM' come from?

Stolpman says on *LifttheVeil,* of this document about the missing people; 'It's a list of people who went missing and then were inducted into S.V.V. it appears, by their tag numbers. S.V.V. R1887 – so that's for the years 1987. You see 7.7. 87 – 33.PSOP. It's hard to say what all this code means but for example, this person Rhonda J. Balcimbe, I mean she's a missing woman and has been missing for 20 years as of 2007. And then we have this sheet here that she was inducted it appears into SVV on July

7th, 1987, and it's every ten years– inductions it seems."

"I'm in an S.V.V. chat room. I hesitate to show it to you because I don't want to lose access but there's a lot of chatter about July 7th. It's interesting. There's what Michael Quinn claims are strong A.I.'s (Artificial Intelligences) such as "Lucy" also known as "Lucifer," and some people called 'Lestat;' all these kinds of demonic nicknames. So, I'm in there and they're talking about July 7th countdown."

"And something really weird is they're talking about a wedding on July 7th of some sort. This S.V.V. follows the Kabbalah so you would have to look at the Kabbalistic meaning of a wedding. Typically, a special joining. Just like you would think, but a spiritual joining between realms perhaps – or between man and the divine. This relates to the puzzle Cicada 3301 which many have

speculated is a recruitment tool perhaps for the S.V.V. or perhaps intelligence services, but if you use the metaphor of a cicada, there is that ten-year cycle when people come out of the induction – the drawing out of."

"So, I don't know if that's when the candidate becomes activated. I believe there's an induction or an 'acquisition' which involves the disappearance, then a programming period, and "psyop camp" I think, - indoctrinating them, in manipulation techniques, spiritual alchemy, changing your reality, and then put them into the secret society system – you can never leave....I'm just putting it out there. I don't know..."

The reader would be advised to see for theirselves. An ARG, a puzzle, a money scam, or something much more sinister?

'What makes one "qualified" to join the

S.V.V.' it asks, on its website. 'Only applicants who reach the Invisible Order will comprehend this. One may behold himself in this Mirror, both within and without, and find What and Who he/she is, may be, or could become. It is a rippling reflection, a glimpse through the Gate of the Mystery of all Beings. What are the benefits of membership? Legion. Being/Becoming.'

It has to be said however, it also adds; Q: What about the conspiracy theories ("I read some articles/saw some videos"?) Answer: Believe what you will. In fact, conspire against us. If you seek Darkness, the Sun will set.' Which would surely mean it is a benign organisation, or is that the wrong way round. Are they saying if you seek darkness, which we are not, you will find darkness as the sun will set, or is it a quip that they are in actuality darkness themselves and so if you seek them you will find them as you wish them to be; darkness?

In the revelation of the possibility of "pizzagate/pedogate" being real, many alternative journalists and researchers have honed in on the topic of missing children and one startling letter was received by researcher Ole Dammegard. Perhaps best known for his work on 'false-flag events,' someone had written to him recently to express his horror at what he had been told by a concerned visitor to a museum at a national park in America.

He revealed this correspondence on former lawyer Alfred Webre's show and he spoke of this strange letter he had received, and which he sent forward to law enforcement investigators, obviously taking it seriously, although of course, we do not know if this is entirely verifiable without knowing the source, the writer themselves. However, if we are to give it due consideration, it would apparently concern a "pedocriminal tunnel holding children at WVA Droop Mountain Museum."

The letter reads as such; 'I met someone who had just returned from the West Virginia Droop Mountain national park. While he was in the Museum he heard children crying out for help. He went to investigate and the children's voices seemed to be coming from the underground as though the museum was built over an underground cavity cave or tunnel.'

Dammegard says, "Thinking that very young children may have been exploring underground in caves and tunnels and got lost, and certain that they were beneath the museum and seeing a possibly sealed entrance into the cavity or tunnel where the children were, he tried to gain entrance. Suddenly two very official looking men in suits came along and told him to move on, He told them that he heard children calling out for help but they said there were no children in the vicinity and told him to leave. The children were still calling, "Please help us!!"

"He said to the two men, "Listen!! You can still hear them!!" but the men escorted him back to his car and watched him leave the park. He tried to involve the police, asking them to accompany him back to the museum but they showed no interest. He had a feeling that they had been told to expect him and to dismiss him. He was already very worried about missing children or being lost under the ground of the museum when pizzagate exploded on the internet."

Alfred Webre says, "We're hypothesising this is a holding area. The children could have been harvested from the visitors to the national park, or gathered up and brought there from the surrounding area through social services agencies, and that it's a central deposit area and then at night the park is shut down and those two men in suits are there and they're either taken out by airplane or an underground tunnel or

railroad. – this could be what we're dealing with."

Ole Dammeguard adds; "National parks are a perfect area to abduct people in- who can you blame? – it's a huge vast area of park!"

But surely, they'd keep them in a warehouse – not somewhere the general public go, such as a museum? Interestingly though, Friars Hole, the longest cave in West Virginia, with eight different entrances and 44 miles of surveyed passage, is apparently located on the western flank of Droop Mountain. All of the entrances of this non-commercial cave are privately owned.

While the experiences of the man at the museum in the national park are perhaps easily explained somehow, perhaps an over-active imagination, or misinterpretation somehow, it also recently came out that there are 1,000's of missing

children in Virginia, (the State in which this Museum is situated) and apparently, the State of Virginia has by far the highest number of missing children per capita across the United States.

Curiously, this person who first noticed this adds that unlike almost all of the other states in the country Virginia provides no photos of nearly all of the missing children. Of 392 missing in Virginia, 202 of them have no photos.

According to this anonymous 'Whistle-blower' called Mark, he discovered a strange pattern in these disappearances too. Of the 202 children missing and without photos, 5 vanished in March, just 1 disappeared in April, 6 vanished without trace in May 7, in June 3, in July 8, it rose to 23 in September, 40 in October, and 74 in November. Why would this be?

The Autumn for Equinox lasts for 13 weeks and for those who believe it, this minor sabbath requires human sacrifice. Samhain, on 31 October to 1 November, also marks the beginning of the "darker half" of the year. Mabon on September 12th is said to be 'one of the illuminati's nights of human sacrifice, as too is Halloween or 'All Hallows Eve.'

Others are more likely to point the finger of blame at organ harvesters and child sex traffickers, rather than any alternative religious practice. Or, is the cause of so many missing children quite simply that the dark mornings and dark evenings of late autumn and the winter months make it far easier for abductions and kidnappings to be carried out under the long hours of darkness rather than the extended daylight and longer days of summer?!

Chapter 6: Monsters we cannot see.

Recently a man contacted me. "I contacted you before about my "predator sighting". I just wanted to let you know that I have just heard your "Invisible Predator" podcast.

Gary had been referring to a podcast in which I mention several eye-witness accounts of what can only really be described as a shimmering, semi-translucent being, for example, Jan's account in one of my previous books 'Predators in the woods,' which was as follows;

'Doctor of Physics Bruce Maccabee, an expert on optics, sounds and lasers at Naval Surface Warfare Centre, and a researcher into ufo's, orbs and other unexplained anomalies describes a case of a 'Predator in the Forest.'

A lady called Jan had set up a hunting stand in her native Ohio at the start of the hunting season. Sitting in the stand about fifteen feet up between the trees in a forested area, she patiently waited.

As she sat there, she passed the time texting friends and taking photos with her phone.

Suddenly the woods went silent. She noticed that there was no noise at all around her; the birds had stopped, there was no rustling in the foliage. Just dead silence. It made her feel suddenly anxious and she was so unnerved by it that she sent a text saying "Something is wrong here. The woods just went dead silent...It's odd."

She thought it was possible a panther or coyote was approaching. As her eyes roamed the area, she suddenly noticed a strange visual effect that seemed to be

moving across her field of vision, about twenty feet away. It looked like a mirage in a desert; but it was not hot there.

She removed her glasses and rubbed her eyes, wondering if something in her eyes was causing it. But when she put her glasses back on it was still there.

It travelled from left to right in front of her, above the ground, and then eventually disappeared from sight. When it did, gradually the animal sounds of the forest returned.

She later described it as 'like the invisible creature in *Predator*.'

Shortly after this, her nephew was at his High School not far away with other students. Several of them there reported seeing strange bright moving lights in the sky as it got dark. They were on their sports field, and the lights were directly above

them, changing colour from white to amber, then they disappeared.

"Airplanes don't just disappear," he said, adding, "Every now and then I felt I could see something out of the corner of my eye, but it was probably my imagination."

Or was it...?
Well, Gary Macrae wanted to explain what had happened to him after hearing me talk about that case. He writes; 'I was utterly shocked that this is going on all over, I had no idea. I have to say that this makes my own sighting even more frightening, as I can no longer brush it off as imagination, although dogs don't imagine things.'

'I am giving you permission to use my story, if you so wish. I can also confirm that I am college educated and, until recently when I became ill, I was a software engineer for 25 plus years. I'm not mentally ill, as some

may suggest and neither is my university educated wife.'

What had happened to Gary you may wonder? Well, "I live in Kirriemuir, Scotland, which is on the edge of the Cairngorms National Park. Please take the time to read this as I think it may be of great interest and you will actually see what I saw. I read a couple of your books on holiday and was fascinated, as there seemed to be a link to several terrifying experiences I had 2-3 years ago. These were not imagination; my wife was involved also and my dogs went ballistic at the entity we saw. Let me explain.'

'Around 4 years ago, I was walking my dogs at night, in the winter on a moon-lit farm track half a mile outside of Kirrimuir. I had a torch but did not have it on due to it being a clear moon-lit evening. To the left of the road, fields drop off sharply towards a small

wooded area for around 200 yards. I was walking along when my dog stopped and something caught my eye.'

'I can only describe this creature/entity as something like Gollom from Lord of The Rings but almost invisible, reflecting the surroundings in the same way as the alien in the Predator films. It was taller than me, about 6-7 feet, at a guess, and it moved quickly towards the top of the hill and easily jumped a fence to end up standing crouched around 50 yards in front of me staring at me, or so it felt as I couldn't actually see the eyes. The dog was already running when I fled. I felt that it chased me but I didn't look back to find out. I ran the mile or so home, locked the doors and told my wife about it.'

'I was pretty shaken by this and we kept it to ourselves. Let's be honest it sounds pretty ridiculous.'

'A good while passed and we had pretty much forgotten about the experiences when the most terrifying one took place. This time we were together with the two dogs, a Labrador and a Standard Poodle, which are pretty large and not easily scared, and back where I had originally sighted the entity but just on our way into the unlit area near some trees. Suddenly the dogs went apoplectic with rage and started barking like devil-dogs, looking up into a tree at the start of the farm track.'

'I shone my torch up and briefly saw the entity again, this time crouched up in the tree. The dogs were going crazy and would not go any further. We about turned and headed home. I did look back and it did not follow us into the lit area.'

'This was terrifying as we now knew that it couldn't be imagination, as the dogs had seen it. I've never seen then so crazy before

that or since that. I could try to describe the fear but really, there are no words.'

'A few weeks passed and we just avoided these areas at night. My wife, Heather then had a daylight sighting. She was just outside of town in another wood one morning when she noticed everything was quiet.'

'She again saw the shimmering shape up in the trees and immediately went home. The dogs didn't seem to notice this time but Heather was quite a bit away from where it was. She didn't go back there alone for a long time afterwards.

'A few months later I was walking my Labrador in the Kirriemuir Den, which is a large un-lit park in the middle of the town. It is like a small valley with trees at the top and bushes dotted around. Again, it was a moonlit night but I was using a torch

because it is very dark in there. I was walking along and had a feeling that I was being watched and the dog seemed uneasy.'

'It all came back to me and I started to sweep the torch around the hillside hoping that nothing was there, but it was running down the hill at an angle towards me, it turned away from me when I shone the CREE torch on it. The torch I use is one of those very powerful night fire models and I saw it very clearly this time.'

'It did run on two legs but also was crouched forward and touched the ground with it's very long arms as it moved. It was definitely the same thing. Around 6-7 feet tall, humanoid, but spindly like Gollum. Reflecting its surroundings. The torch shone brightly off the surface of its skin. I say skin because I don't think it was wearing anything.'

'Both myself and the dog ran like hell, out of the park and into the centre of the town. Again, although it had seen me it ran away from me when I shone the torch on it. After this I did tell a few people, I have a friend whose house backs onto this park, but nobody had heard of it or seen it.'

'As an addition to this, last year one of my friends was in another wood near the town (Caddam Woods) and his Rhodesian Ridgeback dog went crazy "at nothing," in his words. It had never acted this way before and has never since. I did not tell him what I had seen before, as I didn't want to cause alarm. I did share this with my friend Alan though, the one who's house backs onto the park mentioned above.'

'The other thing I wanted to do was to send you a photo I took last year. We were in the woods, near where my wife saw the "predator" in a tree, and I felt that we were

being followed. I also noticed that the dogs were keen to move on more quickly than usual. This time I saw nothing at all, I just had that feeling. It's like a shadow suddenly passes over your soul and you know something is wrong.'

'I snapped a photo behind me and later noticed this weird rectangular, translucent object to the right. I won't circle it. I'll let you see it for yourself. You will have to zoom in to the right a bit. I'm sending it to you as I don't know who to show it to. I thought that you may know someone who can make a suggestion as what it is. The photo was taken with the sun behind me without a flash. I also see something else in that box, which I pray to god is pareidolia. The something else was pointed out to me by a friend.'

'Being a surviving "prey" of the invisible predator myself, I can tell you that this is

nothing from our world. To protect you, these entities cannot stand bright light. Shine a CREE torch at them if you are unlucky enough to come across one. If you have dogs then they are an early indicator that something is wrong. My dogs went apoplectic when they saw the "predator", it was up in a tree.'

'It is hard to spot. If you suspect something then stand deadly still and look around you. You can definitely see it if it moves, the effect is literally like the Predator film. Like a reflection on water or a distortion of light. Whatever I saw was roughly 6-7 ft. tall. It moved extremely fast; you cannot outrun it. Also, you can only see the shape, not the features. Never go out in the woods without a CREE torch of some sort, even in daylight. I hope that none of you ever see this. It is truly horrific. Terrifying."

'With regard to the original photo

(PA160028) and the two close-ups, I fear it is not pareidolia. Something is definitely wrong there. I am not a photography expert but I do collect "vintage digital" cameras, I have around 25, and I am pretty good at telling what camera took which picture. The camera used here, an Olympus u700, is not prone to "artefacts", so if it looks wrong then I would say it is....'

A very odd event occurred in August 1972, at Roachdale, Indiana, at the trailer home of a family called the Rogers, in Roachdale Indiana. The events appeared to begin when a glowing object was seen hovering in the sky above a cornfield close-by. After this, for several nights in a row, the family would hear strange noises in their yard. Randy Rogers went outside to investigate one night, and it was then that he came face to face with something in the cornfield.

Dark, shadowy but appearing solid, the

closest thing it resembled was a gorilla in the darkness of the night. It was upright, although it ran on all fours. On another night, it ventured up to the family's trailer, and Mrs Rogers had the frightful experience of seeing a face staring at her outside the window. She said it stood as a man would stand. The strangest thing was, when the family would look for its tracks and path the next day, they could never find any trace of the creature.

Although they could see that the creature appeared to be covered in dark hair, in the day-time all trace that it had ever visited them was gone. It was as though it had no substance. Apparently, the family told investigators Janet and Colin Bord; "What was so weird was that we never could find any tracks, even when there was mud. It would run and jump but somehow it wasn't touching anything, and when it ran through the weeds you couldn't hear anything.

Sometimes when you looked at it, you could see through it." It appeared almost translucent.

This family were not the only ones who were witness to this oddity. Although it did not appear to harm the family, for a near-by farmer, it led to the mass death of his live-stock. Dozens of his chickens were found mutilated. They had not been "eaten;" they had been "mutilated," and their bodies lay strewn. Grass around them was flattened trodden down. The family quickly summoned the town's Marshall, Leroy Cloncs, who arrived promptly at the urgency of the farming family.

Surveying the animal destruction, he stood with the family outside, discussing the incident when they heard noises not far off. The Marshall quickly got back in his car to drive to the source of the noises, the farmer following close behind on foot.

As the car drove past a certain spot something huge lept out of the ditch by the path and ran behind the car, in front of the farmer, extremely fast. All the farmer saw was a huge dark shape moving at great speed. He later said; "It ran so fast. The fence it ran at was smashed all the way to the ground."

It ploughed straight through the fence and continued on its path running fast. Or so they thought...when the men returned to the farm, as they stood looking out from the door of the farmhouse, it could be seen, towering in the entrance to the chicken house. It had returned. The measurements of the door entrance were 6by8. It completely blocked the view of the inside. In fact, Burdine said, "Its shoulders came up to the top of the door, up to where the neck should have been. But it didn't have a neck. It was groaning. I never saw its face."

He, and the other men of the family grabbed their guns and shot at it, and yet, though the range was only a short distance and they were all certain they had hit it, it escaped and appeared completely uninjured.

This time, whatever it was, it had killed one hundred and ten chickens, all of them ripped apart, drained of blood, and strewn everywhere. Before this all happened, there had been strange lights seen in the sky for a number of nights.

Recently I also corresponded with a man called Jeffrey. 'I'm from Parkersburg West Virginia, I hunt, fish, shoot and spend a lot of time outdoors. I really don't believe any of this crap either but last week something happened that I can't explain. On my way hunting at 6.30 am, driving on lost pavement road something crossed the road in front of me, had to be at least 15ft. tall and

was a medium dark brown in colour. It glided across the road just off the ground."

"When I say crossed, I don't mean walked - it kind of glided quickly as if hovering just off the ground. It was very tall, brown and flew across the road so quickly that I really didn't see detail. All I know is, I have no idea what that was and have never seen anything like it. It was shifting rectangle in shape is best I can describe. I still can't even think what that was and I practically live in the woods."

Jeffrey gave me permission to include our conversation in this book. For those who have read any of my other books, you will have come across sightings and encounters of what seem to be shimmering, almost transluscent 'monsters' for want of a better word and the people have had the misfortune to run into them. We do no know what they are, but, just as in the case of

Gary Macree, they generate a terrible sense of diquiet and fear.

Jeffrey has been a hunter all his life. He is very used to going out into the woods alone, at any hour day or night. He said, "When it happened my first and only thought was "what the hell was that" and I still can't rationalize it."

I asked him, did it have any substance to it or could you see right through it?

"Yes, it was a shifting dark brown shape that hovered quickly across the road. If you have ever seen a flock of birds tightly grouped together it moved like that. You could not see through it. It had a shape and I don't think my mind even accepted what I saw. It scared the hell out of me then. I thought that couldn't be real and tried to dismiss it. Does that make any sense?"

"Yes, it does, though what it was I do not know. But I have found other people who have had similar experiences. Almost as though something was shifting in density." I asked him, "Was there any possible shape to it at all, in terms of any formation of a head or limbs or was it completely blurred?"

"I was expecting to see deer cross the road and when it happened I was like; "What the hell was that? That was no deer, it wasn't birds, whatever it was it was big n fast n it scared me. I don't scare easily or even believe in this kind of thing. Like I said, it happened real fast. I think my mind kind of went into a kind of shock and just couldn't accept what I just saw. All I know is it was a very large creature that hovered across the road was very fast. Never seen anything like it."

I said, "If you could make a guess - what do you think you would say it was? - or came

from? do you think it was a biological entity?"

"I cannot explain and don't even know if I want to. My impression of it was it was evil."

"Do you think it was aware of your presence?"

"There is no way that was a living creature - it was too big and it moved like nothing I ever saw, yet there it was. I don't know, like I said it scared me and my first thoughts was that it was evil. Yes, it knew I was there and was in a hurry to leave."

"So it had an intelligence - to be able to know you were there - This is an impossible question I know - but, what do you think it could have been capable of doing, to you? something physical? or mental?"

"It inspired instant fear and shock to the point that you just didn't want to believe what you just saw, but after it was gone that sense of fear and terror went with it."

"Has it made you concerned when you go

hunting now or have you shrugged it off?" "I'm not one of those people that think humans can know all of what exists, it didn't harm me or even act as if it wanted to - it just was in a hurry to leave. Things exist that we can't explain. I just chalk it up to that. I'm not afraid. Just curious. You can use my name I don't care. It happened, it was a real thing, people that know me know I'm not one to be full of s.... Good luck."

A while after talking with Jeffrey, he contacted me again. He asked me, "Did you see the short video I posted on YouTube? I didn't think about it when we last spoke but the area where I sighted this "Thing" is right next to a graveyard and a very old church. This area is very isolated."

On the video he adds, "Well, this is right where I saw that thing cross the road. Right in this corner here... this is Pleasant Hill Church established 1881 been here forever

and right across is Pleasant Hill cemetery. It's pretty high here and it's pretty windy. Right down there where those pine trees are and that speed limit sign is where it crossed the road in front of me."

"It come up out of that hollow and down over to the right there its real deep back in there and there's a pond down in there but it crossed the road and went over near where that house and yard is and down through that field and disappeared real quick, so, I don't know what it was. Some people are trying to say it's the Mothman. We're 25 miles from Mount Pleasant where the Mothman is from. I don't know... guess we'll never know."

A commentator on it says; - 'If one reads about the Salem witch trials from the people who were there it was not just a case of overzealous Christians. Some of those people were mixed up in some pretty nasty dark

magic. Maybe something similar happened there at some point and let something loose.' Maybe this person has a point...

After I uploading the video to YouTube of myself talking about sightings of these 'invisible' shimmering predator- type entities, https://www.youtube.com/watch?v=Gs1pDJko2J0&t=785s a lady commented on her own experience.

Kristina Wheeler wrote; 'last night, myself and my spouse were surprised by an entity that I could see moving but I could also see through it, I could hear its steps, I could make out the outline sort of ...like water moving in an upright position... it was walking and about 20 yards away from me. I was alone at that point. When my spouse joined me, I told him I thought I'd seen someone up at the top of the road. He said, well back up the car and I'll investigate. I

didn't tell him at that point what I thought that this thing looked like. After I'd picked him I asked if he'd seen anything. He told me what he'd seen... describing it exactly like I had seen...'

'I was in shock for the fact that he saw it too just as I did, except he'd seen it ten minutes prior to my experience up where we were hiking... but I was always in front of him. I didn't even hear him call my name. But anyway, the important thing was that I wasn't seeing things.... I really did see this predator like thing. Seemed to be cloaked in the surrounding elements. So strange I have a million questions!! He won't talk about it. . . but I can't stop thinking about it. I must have answers. I love the woods hiking and all that. I am afraid to go back out there. this is not okay with me.......'

.............I hope you enjoyed this book. If you have had a creepy, strange, or inexplicable experience, please do feel free to contact

me. I am actively continuing to research & collect the strangest of stories. These intriguing cases are just the beginning...... there are many others in the collection of books I've written...

Added to this, I have now started a Podcast, called "Masquerade Podcast with Steph Young:" If you would like to, you can listen to Episodes on iTunes, or here; New Exclusive Episodes will also be available only here;
https://www.patreon.com/stephyoungpodcast
I have a website;
http://www.stephyoungauthor.com/
if you would like to subscribe to my mailing list, to stay up to date with new releases.

I hope you have enjoyed this book and the strange collection of mysterious events. If you have enjoyed it, perhaps you would be

kind enough to leave me a review, Thank you so much, Steph.

Excerpts – From 'Dead in the Water: Forever Awake.'

Introduction:

Hundreds of young men; vanishing without a trace, only for many of them to be found dead; weeks or months later, in remote rivers or creeks, shallow ponds or canals, in areas that search parties have searched multiple times before; their bodies later discovered there, as though placed to be found.

There is something very sinister happening to college-age men. It has been going on since the early '90's, and quite likely since before then. What's more, it isn't stopping; it appears to be escalating, and no-one knows why.

Young men attending college are going missing; the numbers are rising, as they disappear in what can only be described as sinister and inexplicable circumstances. Then they are found dead; always in water, often very shallow water.

"The naughty boys, well....they go directly into the shallow water. And then, they are all gone...no ghost, no memories...as if they never lived in the first place. And then they stay there; awake and afraid."

"The evil is rampant and deep and wide-spread. He was tortured, taken to the river and killed. Then his body was 'positioned' and taken to a different part of the water."
"Nobody will speculate on the disappearances because they don't understand the sinister nature of the world they are living in. This is dark alchemy indeed."

"Once so vital, he is now.....grist for the

mill. For a machine.....A machine full of teeth he never saw coming."

"We take what we need and leave. Understand this: This is necessary. Life feeds on life feeds on life feeds on death feeds on life."

"If people knew the depth of this, they would be terrified to be outside at night, whether out in the country or in the city."

Chapter 1:

"By the time you read this message I'll be sinking into the ocean ...ending my time in this wretched life. On this day I can finally see the ones I've seeked all these years. Finally Toader Cazazu can..."

This was the last post on Toader Cazacu's facebook. At the time of writing this book, in February 2016, to the shock of his friends who had seen him just thirty minutes prior to him posting this message on facebook, Toader is missing. He has not posted anything since, and his fate is not known. Is it strange that he used his full name?

Could Toader's message about sinking into the ocean, tie in with what could be construed as a taunting message in a forum, even though the message was posted years before? It was posted from a Japanese i.p. address; perfect for concealing a person's true location, and was posted in response to a thread trying to solve the mystery behind the ever growing number of young men who are being found dead in the water.

"Can't believe I missed this for 4 years! Your theory is sound; too bad all of that work for nothing. Slight problem; just like the night good ol' Jack got two in one night and was almost caught; work unfinished. Alchemy? Transcendence of the soul/spirit/ consciousness. My brother Germain has seen the hypocrisy, the pure greed and the lies conveyed at Nicea. We take what we need and leave. Understand this: This is necessary. Life feeds on life feeds on life feeds on death feeds on life. We will never leave; just sink back to where we came from :)"

Is this a joke? Or, does it hold vital clues? It's something we will look deeply into as this book progresses.

Two hours away, and one day before Toader posted his message on facebook about 'sinking into the ocean,' Harvard student Zachary Marr disappeared while out with his cousins at a Bar in Boston. He was not allowed back into the Bar after going outside for a cigarette. The Bar dispute this. Again at the time of writing, the police released a statement saying that they believe the surveillance cameras show him as he enters the ice cold Charles River. It was a cold night in Boston, in February. Why would a young man go down to the River and get into the water? He had only gone outside the Bar to have a quick cigarette.

In that same stretch of water, two weeks before Zachary disappeared, Matthew Genovese also disappeared after leaving a bar. His co-workers, who were in the bar with him, said that he did not appear to be intoxicated. On January 23rd, 2016, Matthew was found dead in the Hudson River. Strangely, his billfold was found on the pier beside the water.

24 days before this, on December 31st, the body of Northeastern University Dennis Njoroge was found in the river. He had disappeared on November 29th. His body was found in Boston's

Charles River on December 31st. Following autopsy and toxicology tests, the city coroner concluded that it was impossible to determine if the young man had drowned by accident or suicide, or if he had "somehow died elsewhere," and was then placed in the water already dead.

The cause and also the manner of the young man's death was therefore listed as "unknown" and the Boston police stated that they were not going to be investigating it. It was determined by them not to be suspicious; despite the fact that from the Coroner's report, he could quite easily have been killed and then placed in the water.

Again in Boston, on February 8, 2014, graduate Eric Munsell was out celebrating his birthday. Eric was in a bar with friends when he was thrown out by a bouncer because, according to his Mother, he had tripped on his way to the bathroom. His body was discovered in the river two months later, at the same spot he was believed to have entered the water, according to cell phone records. A passer-by had seen his "non-viable" body floating in the water. Why had his body not been seen before? Had he been in the water for 2 months, or not?

On Christmas day 2015, the body of Lehman College student Anthony Urena was found dead in the same stretch of water. It was believed his body had drifted from the Harlem River, into the New Jersey side of the Hudson River, where he was recovered. He had last been seen leaving a nightclub in New York City around 5 a.m. He had been missing for six weeks. At this point in time, it is not known if he had been in the water the entire time; or "elsewhere" for some of the time he had been missing.

Indiana student Joseph Smedly was found dead in the water in Griffy Lake, north of Bloomington, on October 2nd, 2015. He'd written on his twitter account; 'If I am found dead; *it won't be suicide*. Perhaps I have said too much." The official autopsy said that he had committed suicide. His sister says he was drowned, with rocks inside the backpack that was strapped to his body when he was found.

Henry McCabe was found partially submerged in a remote body of water on November 2nd, 2015. He had disappeared on Labor Day, September 7th, 2015, in Minnesota. On the night he disappeared, he left what can only be described as the most haunting, most chilling, and most harrowing voicemail, after he went missing. He is screaming, pleading and growling in raw, animalistic agony. Disturbingly, in the background, is something that sounds mechanical. Even more horrific, a voice then interrupts his screams and calmly tells him, in a cold, emotionless, detached voice, "Stop it."

He was found in the water seven miles from where he was last known to have been on the night he disappeared. His body bore no signs of trauma; and yet it had sounded as though he was being tortured. How does that make any sense?

What could have been happening to him on that terrible night?

His Mother says, "This is what they did to my son. Someone killed my son. Before Henry died, he was pleading to someone who dropped him in the dark... Henry paid for you to learn the lesson... When he got off from that car in that morning, he had no idea that he was going to die..."

She seems to be suggesting here that Henry was 'delivered' to his terrible fate; as though he was offered up in some form of sacrifice, in some form of pre-planned killing. Rather bizarrely however, the police, despite his harrowing blood-curdling voicemail, say that they do not think there was any foul play involved. He had been missing for 5 days.

An elder in the Twin Cities' Liberian community, of which Mr McCabe was one, commented, "He can't have got here all by himself," to a location that he pointed out is very isolated, very remote, and dark after 6 pm. "Someone dropped him in the water." The Elder made the statement that the police should not overlook the possibility that his death was connected to violence in his home country, where he had endured a life enmeshed in more than a decade of civil war. On the other hand, his death bears remarkable and uncanny similarities to the many other young men being found drowned, who have not come from Liberia to America; who were all-round 'All American' boys....And many of them also made very disturbing phone calls just before they died or were taken, and were then found dead, days or weeks later, in bodies of water. What is perplexing, and very worrying, is that none of these cases are being investigated as suspicious.

We have the terrible case of Walton Ward. His sister says her brother also died in inexplicable, mysterious and terrible circumstances.

"Walton was last seen alive at Landsharks Bar, Indianapolis, with a 'bouncer' at approximately 1:20-1:30 a.m. on October 12, 2012. His last attempt to save his own life was at 1:30 a.m. when he dialled 911 from his Phone for help. His killers interrupted his 911 call and murdered him...He knew he was going to be killed. His desperate call lasted for 1 second, which was just enough to register to the nearest cell phone tower...but it wasn't not long enough to save his life."

"That was the last time we know him to be alive, until construction workers discovered his body on October 22, floating in the River a few blocks from the bar 10 days after his desperate call to 911 on that night. His phone was found on the bank of the River behind a Restaurant. The police said he must have been 'drunk', 'fallen in' or 'gone swimming' in the dead of winter."

Other victims, who have ended up dead, the same way, have left comments on their facebook or twitter accounts, that also clearly cry out for investigation. Whether overtly or cryptically, some of these victims are in need of help even before they have disappeared. Something very strange, very alarming, and very sinister is going on.

Why did one young man write this on his facebook page, within hours of his death?
"Not afraid of death cause I'm so curious of what's next."
The answer may not be the most obvious one, as we will later examine. It was the last post on Mason Cox's facebook page. A week later, his body was found in a river, along with the body of his best friend. It was officially classified as 'accidental drowning.' Both autopsies determined that they had died from "accidental drowning compounded by hypothermia," according to Sherry Lang, spokeswoman for the Georgia Medical Examiner.

His Mother however, has a different version. "My son was beaten, teeth missing, blunt trauma to the back of his head. His eyes so horrible... His stomach black and blue."

As one victim said before he died, "When you really look into the mystery and the place and the settings and the symbolism, you're f...d, yeah .....It's far too upsetting. Far too unknown."

It's not known explicitly if he was referring to these deaths; however, something was clearly troubling him, something which had led him to seek mental health assistance for the first time in his life, just days before he disappeared. Why did this student, Jake Nawn, make a video in which he says these words, and post it on his facebook, just days before he was found dead in a river near his Plymouth State Campus on November 17th, 2015.

Was he talking about something an outside observer could not understand; about a harmless topic only known by his friends? Or, was he hinting at some kind of desperate trouble he had unwittingly got himself into?

As will later be explored; there are themes here which quite possibly point to more than just a human hand in these disappearances and deaths. Something that is quite possibly so dark, so arcane and alchemical, that it belongs in the realm of rituals which go back centuries. Something that belongs in a dimension of the darkest black magic; and yet something that runs from the lowest echelons to the highest. A slick operation of willing accomplices, lured into a pact which seeks to serve only their higher masters. Allegiances run deep and for now, they remain unbroken.

Jake vanished inexplicably when he had been due to meet his family after class. It was to be five days until searchers spotted his body in the water of the Pemigewasset River. His autopsy determined that he had drowned, although the coroner said, "the exact manner of death will remain undetermined."

In 2011, Mike Shaw wrote of the grief, the anger and the sense of helplessness he felt because he could not save his best friend.

"Sly McCurry did not walk out onto the ice of Lake Superior (Wisconsin) that cold January (2010) winter night and fall through and drown. He was murdered. No one can ever convince me it was anything but murder. He was more than a friend to me. His smile would light up a room. He was always full of life, always happy. He would never have went from the Nightclub to that secluded area alone in 20 degrees below weather, with no coat, and drown. He had no car and after being thrown out of the club via the back door, on the alleged grounds that he was drunk, he was left in the alleyway. Four months later, his body was found in the lake. I was a trained fighter for many years and felt protective over my friends. I have never received closure. His death was ruled "accidental due to cold water immersion." His scent stopped at the back door of the hotel. Like clockwork, I see this killers strike all over the North-East."

College boys are going missing; later to be found drowned. Not all have drowned in the water;

some have drowned elsewhere. According to Ret'd NYPD Kevin Gannon, "They have been abducted, held sometimes for an extended amount of time, mentally tortured, killed, and then placed in the water."

"The evil is rampant and deep and widespread. He was tortured, taken to the river and killed. Then his body was 'positioned' and taken to a different part of the water," says one of the victim's mothers.

The victim type is almost always the same; athletic, popular, high achieving white male college students who go missing after a night out drinking with friends. Choosing to go home, instead of walking back with friends later, or more often, being 'kicked out' of bars, on what later appear quite possibly to be fabricated reasons; they then disappear, only to be found some time later, drowned in nearby rivers or creeks or ponds; even retention tanks.

Many will say they were drunk and disoriented and fell in the river. Many will say inevitably, that the reason they are all of a similar victimology is because more young men than women would choose to walk off alone at night. They will say that they are popular college kids who are letting off steam, drinking too much, and then underestimating how much they have drunk, and as a result they get into difficulty when walking home.

Others however, will ask why they would choose to walk away from their direct route home, often for a long distance, to a river or creek or shallow pond, usually in the middle of winter, without coats, and 'go for a swim' or 'fall in,' rather than go straight home. This is the same scenario for almost all of the victims.

The majority of them were former lifeguards, or on swim teams, well-built and in excellent shape, many excelling as athletes as well as academics; and most of them were not known to be particularly heavy drinkers. They were all highly intelligent, and understandably not prone to jumping onto rivers and lakes in freezing temperatures, on their own, late at night, miles away from home.

Hundreds of young men vanishing without a trace, only for many of them to be found dead, weeks or months later, in remote rivers or creeks, shallow ponds or canals; or in rivers very close to where they were last seen, in areas that search parties have thoroughly searched many times before; their bodies then discovered as though placed there to be found.

Boys are disappearing on the same day across different states, even different countries. There is never any sign of a struggle. There are never any signs of foul play. They are often seen in the presence of unknown strangers, often young, prior to their vanishing.

Always men, always high achievers, always excellent swimmers, always in the colder months. Almost all are kicked out of bars, purposely separated from their friends, made vulnerable and alone and left to their fate.

Why are young men being found drowned, either in water that is only a few feet deep? Or found in remote bodies of water, in areas that the young men would never have been heading to? Some are even found in areas one would think are completely inaccessible.

On October 7, 2010, officials confirmed that they had recovered the body of missing Western University Student Dwight Clark, who had vanished 12 days earlier after leaving a party at around 2 a.m. He was discovered about 1 km from the party, in a log lagoon, which was gated and locked. His friends said he did not appear drunk when he left.

Why and how would he have got into that private property in the first place? Oddly, a blank message was sent from his phone, shortly after he disappeared. The location the message came from was an entirely different location to the one he was found in.

The official story from law enforcement is always that they have 'accidentally drowned,' yet somehow and inexplicably they have often done this in very shallow water. They are, according to the official versions, supposed to have walked miles or many blocks, in the wrong direction, until they reach a remote body of water, and then drowned.

Curiously, some of them have been in towns they have never visited until that night, only to be found in remote ponds that they could never have known even existed, nor the route to take to get to them. Alternately, they appear to have scaled fences or other difficult obstacles to get into remote ponds and then drowned in water that is no deeper than a couple of feet.

Are there any clues which could help explain what has happened to these young men, and why?

Why are many of them found missing one shoe?
Why are their cell phones often found beside the river's edge, again as though purposely placed there?
Why have some of their bodies been 'placed' into positions which are wholly inconsistent with that of a drowning victim?

Someone who drowns will usually be found floating face down in the water. One victim was on his back and had his arms crossed over his body. Another was 'bobbing' up in the water in an upright position. Another was held in place by two small sticks; 'displayed' there waiting to be found.

Why have some of the bodies been found 'half-in and half-out' of the water? Like Henry McCabe, like Mike Knolls.
Why do some of the toxicology reports show drugs that the boys were never known to have taken?
Why have they not fought back or struggled? Very often, they have no injuries whatsoever;

indicating that they have not struggled, even though they were drowning. Obviously the very sinister implication here then is that they were either unconscious or dead when they entered the water. Some even have no water at all in their lungs; yet they have apparently "drowned" in the water.

Drowning in water is not a common suicide method, with less than 4% of men choosing this method. In fact, it's especially difficult to commit suicide in shallow water, and furthermore, it would require weighing oneself down to make the body heavier.

The bodies when found, are often not in the state in which they would be expected to be found. Sometimes their deaths are 'inconclusive,' or 'undetermined.' Sometimes the pathologists openly rule that the cause of death will probably never be determined; which is itself highly alarming given that law enforcement then refuse to follow up on the cases and investigate them.

They are just said to have simply drowned, *somehow*.

The original retired detectives who investigated over a decade ago, found that in some of these cases, the young men had been held, drugged, mentally tortured, physically tortured, killed, and then taken to the water and placed in it.

Strangely, a common factor is that many times the young men have been seen in the presence of not only unknown young people, but cops and bouncers too. Nothing strange there perhaps; but maybe it's not that clear cut.

Several of the men have even phoned friends to say that 'someone' or 'people' are after them, that they are in fear for their lives and that they 'haven't done anything wrong.' Who is after them? And does this implicate the police, or perhaps people pretending to be the police?

Why are there other stories floating around of

possible 'near misses,' in which the young men describe attempts by strangers to lure them outside? Why do some of the parents of the deceased young men talk about the 'unknown' people being at the scene of their disappearance? Of strangers chasing them, and of being terrified for their lives?

Why do many of them make desperate phone calls just moments before something happens to them?
Why are some of them in such a state of terror or horror when they phone their parents or friends?
Why would their cell phones suddenly go dead after they have said something very disturbing?
What are they seeing, in the final moments before their phone is cut off?
Why are they later found in places searched multiple times before?
Why are their bodies 'placed' in strange positions, as though arranged by someone?
Why are many missing one shoe?
Why do few of them have any signs of injury?

What did one boy mean, "Look in the periodic table" before he vanished?

Why is graffiti sometimes found referring to Hydrogen? Hydrogen originates from the Greek word, 'Genes, genetics, and DNA.'

Why does a leading criminologist say, "This is terrorism; they operate as cells." But, it's not terrorism as we usually understand it; it's something very, very different.

How could this have anything to do with the alleged occurrences of 'false flags?' or 'black ops'?

Why did one boy's scent track to an Abbey in an area he had never been to while alive? Why were priests at that Abbey describing an occult drowning ritual on an esoteric forum? This is just the beginning of one possibility...

What does a taunting message posted in a forum referring to a man who is said to be immortal, mean?

Are the people who are doing this communicating online? Are cryptic or bragging messages being left that we have overlooked?

Is this all hyperbole and exaggeration? Is it looking for things that simply aren't happening? Or, does a very unusual cabal exist, that no-one would ever have thought of; obsessed with both deliverance and immortality, and the evidence suggests they are more powerful than the illuminati? They believe they cannot be caught. They believe they are above reproach; they believe they are untouchable.

Or, is the simplest answer; drink and misadventure? Vance Holmes, who runs the blog 'Drowning in Coincidence' and who has followed these cases when they were first believed to have started, asks in one of the cases, how the young man would even have been capable of getting to the river in which he was found drowned, given his intoxication. Calling it "too drunk to drown," his says, of 21 year old Lucas Homan, how did he end up dead in the Mississippi river?

"I understand he may have been drinking. I understand he may have stumbled away from his friends unnoticed. I understand that at the water's edge, he may have accidentally fallen in. What I don't understand is how he got to the river in the first place. His blood alcohol was 0.32 %."

Holmes then quotes from a guide, provided by a breath-testing company, citing the symptoms of anyone who has a blood alcohol reading in the range of 0.25- 0.40 %. They are as follows; 'Inability to stand or walk, stupor, loss of motor functions, impaired consciousness; sleep or stupor.'

"How then did Lucas get to the river at all?"

The estimated number of cases is now well over 300, according to profilers. The predominant cases are those where young men have been 'kicked out' of bars by bouncers, yet it later turns out, they have invariably been wrongly accused of being drunk or disorderly. Then they are found dead in water, days, weeks, or even months later, usually in areas where searches have occurred multiple times. Some have been drinking and are drunk; many others are not drunk in any way, with no alcohol in their system.

Curiously, there are other cases that are even stranger. How do some of the young men end up extremely drunk to the point of nausea and disorientation, so quickly once inside a bar? Those who have been found to be drunk, are excessively 'drunk;' so much so that it would seem impossible for them to have walked to the remote water where they are found dead weeks or months later.

Many have appeared so disoriented and confused that they have had to leave the Bar or Party they are attending. Some have later been found to have had drugs in their system; drugs their close friends knew they never took. Again, it can easily be dismissed as youth and misadventure; but there have been many cases where disorientation takes place so quickly and so suddenly that the suggestion is their drinks are being tampered with. Moreover, when the men are later found dead in the water, there have been several cases where MDMA or GHB or sedatives have been found in their systems. None of the young men were ever known to have taken these drugs nor were they being prescribed sedatives.

How does a young man appear fine one moment, disoriented and confused the next, then suddenly disappear, and then end up dead in water that is only a couple of feet deep? Why can he not be found for often what amounts to weeks? Why would he go to the most remote body of water, always in the opposite direction to that which he was heading?

Of the ones who were kicked out, very often for reasons which are either spurious and false, or later flatly denied, why are these boys purposely 'separated' from their friends; isolated and made vulnerable, often left outside without their wallets or coats, in winter, and then later found in bodies of water? In almost every case, why have even those who have had nothing to drink, walked in the exact opposite direction to that which they told their friends they were heading, back to their home?

How do they then end up dead in water, often having apparently climbed over high fences and 'jumped' into ponds or retention tanks, just a few inches deep, and 'forgotten how to swim?' How do very fit wrestlers, sportsmen, and most notably, boys on swim teams, end up dead in shallow water, only inches deep, having suddenly become unable to swim?

Why have they then often made very disturbing phone calls after they disappear? Why are several of them screaming down the phone before it goes dead? What are they seeing? Who or what is there, with them? Who is taking them? And why? And where are the missing ones who are never found?

End of excerpt

I hope you enjoyed this collection. If you have had a creepy, strange, or inexplicable experience, do feel free to contact me. I am actively continuing to research & collect the strangest of stories.

These intriguing cases are just the beginning...... there are many others in the collection of books I've written....

Added to this, I have now started a Podcast, called "Masquerade Podcast with Steph Young:" If you would like to, you can listen to Episodes on iTunes, or here; **New Exclusive Episodes will also be available only here; https://www.patreon.com/stephyoungpodcast**

I have a website; **http://www.stephyoungauthor.com/** if you would like to subscribe to my mailing list, to stay up to date with new releases.

I hope you have enjoyed this book and the strange collection of mysterious events. If you have enjoyed it, perhaps you would be kind enough to leave me a review, Thank you so much, Steph.

48052349R00127

Made in the USA
Columbia, SC
05 January 2019